When We Get to Heaven

Runaway Slaves on the Road to Peterboro

Norman K. Dann

LOG CABIN BOOKS
HAMILTON, NY

Log Cabin Books, Hamilton, NY 13346
© Copyright 2008 by Norman K. Dann
All rights reserved. Published 2008
First Edition
Printed in the United States of America

Library of Congress Control Number: 2008922849

Dann, Norman K.
A brief history of the slavery in America. The Underground Railroad and the passage of slaves along that trail and through Peterboro, NY, home of the National Abolition Hall of Fame & Museum.
Includes bibliographical references.
Includes index.
ISBN No. 978-0-9755548-4-5
1. Underground Railroad.   2. Peterboro, NY.
3. Slavery in America.   4. The antebellum period in America.

Edited by Brian L. McDowell
Research and contributions by Donna Dorrance Burdick,
Historian, Town of Smithfield, Madison County, NY

*The publisher will donate a portion of the proceeds
from the sale of this book to the
National Abolition Hall of Fame & Museum*

Cover photo: The east facade of the Smith mansion in Peterboro, NY. The mansion was an important stop on the Underground Railroad.
Photo courtesy of the National Abolition Hall of Fame

This book is dedicated to my wife, Dorothy Willsey-Dann, who provided the original spark of inspiration for me to research the abolition movement.

Contents

Preface
1

Part I: Slave Life on the Plantation

One
The Power of Freedom
5

Two
Slavery and the Law
13

Three
Free Labor versus Slave Labor
and the Culture of the South
23

Four
Slave Life
37

Five
Punishment of Resistance
49

Six
Rebellion and Escape
57

Part II: On the Road

Seven
The Runaway Slave
67

Eight
Station Masters, Conductors,
and Passengers
75

Nine
Fugitive Slave Laws
and Northern Prejudice
89

Part III: Runaways in Peterboro

Ten
Attitudes and Connections
103

Eleven
Former Slaves in Peterboro
115

End Notes
141

Bibliography
155

Index
163

About the Author
170

Preface

This book is written not for the scholar of the antebellum era, but for anyone who is interested in the complex web of social structures, issues, and practices that led to and supported the Underground Railroad. It documents in a general sense the relationship between slavery and the Underground Railroad. More specifically, it details the effects slavery had on the hamlet of Peterboro, New York—and how events that originated in this small, rural community in Central New York profoundly altered the lives of many people on either side of the slavery issue.

This three-section book begins with a look at slavery on the Southern plantation, examining the social system that compelled many slaves to attempt escape. Part II examines the runaway slaves' experiences "on the road" north as they continued their flights to freedom amid unthinkable hardships. Part III documents what we know about the experience of some individual fugitive slaves as they passed through the hamlet of Peterboro, using the Underground Railroad station there operated by abolitionist Gerrit Smith and his family and associates.

While Parts I and II rely heavily on secondary sources, Part III is based on original source material researched by the author and his colleague in research, Town of Smithfield Historian Donna Dorrance Burdick. I feel indebted to Donna for her tireless efforts to research specific details of the trials of individual former slaves as they traveled through Peterboro.

Those who study the antislavery movement of the 1800s know that the end of slavery in America did not bring with it the end of racial inequality. Slaves who attained freedom by escaping the South quickly learned that discrimination against them in the North was often as much of a deterrent to their personal and economic successes as had been slavery in the South. In some ways, that discrimination survives to this day.

A word about language: While I respect the recent tendency in Underground Railroad scholarship to cleanse the readers' minds of notions of slavery as applied to "fugitive" or "runaway" escapees, I find the term "freedom seeker" to be too general a reference. I challenge writers to find for me anyone who is *not* a "freedom seeker." Certainly if my freedom were threatened, I would be motivated to immediate and vigorous action.

Therefore, in this book, I do at times refer to "fugitive slaves" and "runaway slaves;" indeed, they did run away from slavery to become fugitives—in terms of southern law.

Near the end of the book, I introduce the reader to the term "freedom seeker" as an alternative conceptualization of those people who escaped from the institution of slavery.

During the Underground Railroad movement, blacks were as important as whites in the struggle for human rights. Today, as the gap between blacks and whites remains and in some cases continues to grow, we can learn a great deal by examining the stories of those people who championed the abolition movement more than 150 years ago.

Racist attitudes strike a raw nerve in *all* of us. Too often, when we might confront those attitudes, we choose to ignore them. By looking closely at the origins of these attitudes and their effects on a nation before and during the Civil War, this book offers insights that may help guide our modern-day thoughts and actions.

Part I

Slave Life on the Plantation

One

The Power of Freedom

"DEATH——death at any time in preference to slavery," said a Kentucky slave in 1829, just before he was hanged for having participated in the killing of his owner.[1]

Certainly this slave saw his own death as a type of freedom. He likely had spent his whole life as a 'thing' instead of a person, being owned, controlled and dominated by someone whom he hated. "Slavery," said Harriet Tubman, "is the next thing to hell."[2]

To take from a human being the power of choice is to deny his basic right to freedom. Throughout human history, this act has been the greatest motivating force behind rebellion—be it on an individual or collective scale. Whether we look at a society rising to war due to "taxation without representation," a family of slaves escaping the ownership of a master, or an entire race fleeing persecution, the dynamic force behind such action is the loss of freedom and the desperate attempts to regain it.

People will leave behind everything—every custom, every possession, and everyone they know—for a breath of freedom. Possessions cannot hold one back; familiar places and customs cannot hold one back; even love for another person cannot deter the quest for freedom.

When We Get to Heaven

A Lake Erie steamboat captain gained a new understanding of the power of freedom as he deposited runaway slaves on a Canadian beach:

> "They seemed to be transformed; a new light shone in their eyes, their tongues were loosed, they laughed and cried, prayed and sang praises, fell upon the ground and kissed it over and over. I thought to myself, 'My God! Is it possible that human beings are kept in such a condition that they are made perfectly happy by being landed and left alone in a strange land with no human beings or habitations in sight, with the prospect of never seeing a friend or relative?' "[3]

Slaves in America probably knew better than any other people in the history of the world the pull of freedom that would lead them away from the greatest social madness ever known. Fleeing the slave owners who bound them, they struck out into a physical and social wilderness full of unknowns. Even the threat of death was not a deterrent.

They had spent their lives shackled to a "peculiar institution" that exploited their existence for the benefit of others. It dulled their minds with intentional ignorance and punished any resistance with mental torture and physical anguish. They were ready to graduate to freedom, their diplomas written in scars on their backs.

A Quiet Beginning

The history of slavery in America began quietly in 1619 when a Dutch ship dropped anchor in the James River in what would become Virginia and sought provisions in exchange for twenty-three Negroes.[4]

The growth of the institution of slavery was not rapid for the first hundred years when the main agricultural crop was tobacco, which could be worked mainly by white indentured servants. During the 1700s, large-scale cultivation of rice and indigo and increased tobacco production encouraged the expansion of Negro slavery. But perhaps the greatest factor in the development of slavery came with Eli Whitney's invention of the cotton gin in 1793. The cotton gin mechanized the production of cotton, thus requiring vastly increased numbers of field workers.[5]

As slavery grew in the developing United States, it brought with it a major change to 'traditional' slavery as it had existed worldwide. Previously, wealth had led to slavery because only the wealthy could afford it; but transplanted Europeans reversed that relationship. The sheer numbers of Africans who were kidnapped from their homeland and brought overseas in crowded ships made slavery quite economical for its practitioners. Soon, slavery in America had become a means of acquiring wealth.

As such, it institutionalized a culture of violence, abuse of the land, lack of appreciation for education, prejudice toward dark skin color, and a bipolar class system that ceded power to a small collection of slave owners.

Whereas some Southerners interpreted this as a natural and good relationship between persons, others warned, as Pierre Lanfrey noted in his writings on Napoleon,

> "Do not misconstrue events, history is not a school of fatalism, but one long plea for the freedom of man."[6]

Indeed, as slavery expanded in the United States, philosophical thinkers popularized the idea of freedom as a natural right of all people. When Thomas Jefferson wrote the preamble to the Declaration of Independence, he understood that the "self-evident" and "inalienable" right to freedom inhered in all persons equally, and—although this contradicted his personal behavior as a slave owner—he argued that it was freedom that should guide the thoughts and actions of the new nation.

But what about slaves? They were already here, and they presented a problem for nation-builders bent on institutionalizing freedom for all. The disgraceful solution of the Constitution's authors was to consider slaves as property—and therefore bereft of rights that applied to people.

When We Get to Heaven

The slaves, these supposedly humane philosophers rationalized, were not to be considered as humans, but as commodities—things to be used for financial return like a horse or a plow. This dehumanized those on both sides, victimizing all to positions from which no one could self-actualize, or realize one's full potential.

For the slaves, the American Revolution was an unfinished fight. They fully understood that one could enslave a body, but not a mind; the irony was that those who had fought bravely against political domination could so willingly institutionalize racial tyranny.

Frederick Douglass felt that tyranny. As a boy, he had been brutalized by a despotic owner. He came to see freedom not only as his natural right, but as a powerful motivating force. Humans, he claimed—slaves and slave holders alike—had to *learn* to abuse freedom.

"Nature has done almost nothing to prepare men and women to be either slaves or slave holders. Nothing

Escaped slave and staunch abolitionist Frederick Douglass, from the portrait by Joe Flores.
Courtesy of the National Abolition Hall of Fame & Museum

but rigid training, long persisted in, can perfect the character of one or the other. One cannot easily forget to love freedom; and it is as hard to cease to respect that natural love in our fellow creatures."[7]

Douglass realized the full social impact of slavery upon a society when he said, "Make a man a slave, and you rob him of moral responsibility."[8] And without moral responsibility on either side, the stage was set for the degradation of basic human interaction on all levels.

Douglass viewed the institution of slavery as containing the seeds of its own demise, because the slave holder—cruel or kind—was a tyrant:

> "[The slave owner is]... every hour the violator of the just and inalienable rights of man; and he is, therefore every hour silently whetting the knife of vengeance for his own throat.... [T]he kindness of the slave master only gilds the chain of slavery, and detracts nothing from its weight or power."[9]

One recent researcher of history has discovered that separation of the family by the owner through sale of one or more of its members was relatively rare because most plantations were small, possessing fewer than twenty slaves, and owners were concerned about keeping families intact. This interpretation of slave family history seems brutal in its own right: How does one reconcile the fact that his family is intact only as a means of economic efficiency? He has already been captured, robbed of culture, forced under threat of death into an alien life and into a work pattern for which there is no pay, no appreciation, and the constant threat of physical punishment and even death.

That historian's statement that "Slave owners were... strong supporters of slave families"[10] seems self-serving at best. The fact that *most* slave families were not intentionally split cannot, as Frederick Douglass put it, soften the blow of bondage.

This claim that an intact slave family allowed slaves to resist the "dehumanization" produced by "instantaneous and unquestioned obedience" owed to masters ignores the significance of the slaves' drive for freedom.[11] If *any* slave families were split, the moral cruelty of the institution of slavery surpassed all crimes. Denying freedom is always a formula for revolution; the wonder is that slave rebellions did not occur in every community.

As one emancipated slave said—even though he was never whipped—"I was cruelly treated because I was kept in slavery."[12] It seems clear that slave owners knew that unless they were tyrannical and cruel, the relentless drive for freedom would win.

A symptom of the slave owner's insensitivity to the slaves' desire for freedom was his surprise at their efforts to escape. Slave owners had difficulty understanding why so many slaves ran away. Even the contented, privileged, skilled, quiet, obedient ones left "for no apparent reason." John Hope Franklin, a researcher of runaway slaves, said of slave owners,

> "It appeared that no matter how diligent, punitive, or lenient, no matter how imaginative, ingenious, or attentive, no matter how determined, compassionate, or brutal, they remained unable to halt the stream of slaves that left their plantations and farms."

Owners often charged that slaves left "without any cause," or "without any unjust or injurious treatment." Even George Washington was surprised when his seamstress slave ran away in 1797. His claim that she had been "brought up and treated more like a child than a Servant" seems to discount the cruelty of slavery.[13]

In trying to rationalize what they regarded as the slaves' inexplicable attempts at escape, some owners assumed their slaves suffered from mental problems. They conjured up conspiracies led by abolitionists in the North or by free blacks in the South.

They could not understand why their runaway slaves would not return.[14]

The chasm that separated such perceptions of slave owners from those of the slaves and many Northerners presaged the conflict of ideas that would define the antebellum reform era. This conflict, which would lead a nation to civil war, was most clearly seen by those who had lived in both worlds. Angelina Grimké, the daughter of a South Carolina slave owner, moved north and became an abolitionist. "There are," she wrote, "only two ways in which [the demise of slavery] can be effected, by moral power or physical force, and it is for [the South] to choose which of these you prefer."[15]

Former Kentucky slave owner James G. Birney, who later would become an abolitionist presidential candidate, wrote in an 1835 letter to Peterboro, NY abolitionist Gerrit Smith,

"The antagonist principles of liberty and slavery have been roused into action and one or the other must be victorious. There will be no cessation of the strife, until slavery shall be exterminated, or liberty destroyed."[16]

To the credit of the Northern states, they tried to abolish the institution of slavery by moral suasion and by the force of law. The culture that arose from the slave trade and the laws that men wrote to respond to that culture both help explain the social, political and economic struggles that dominated the nineteenth century.

Two

Slavery and the Law

The African slave trade represents one of the cruelest episodes in all of human history. Black Africans were perceived as innately inferior beings by white Europeans. Even their skin color fed this perception: for centuries in European culture, the color black had symbolized "dirt, laziness, ugliness, sexual perversion and sin." The black male was therefore regarded as "bestial or brutish."[1]

This symbolism translated into fear and hatred of blacks, and it precluded any hope of their integration into European society. The trade for slaves during the four hundred years between 1450 and 1850 brought nearly eleven million Africans to the Western Hemisphere, of which only one-half million came to the territory now called the United States. The other ten and one-half million went to South America, Central America, and the Caribbean area.[2]

The means by which Africans were delivered into slavery in these new worlds were indications of the inhuman treatment they could expect for the rest of their enslaved lives.

The ocean journey was difficult. Many slaves died enroute because of physical abuse. Those who survived faced social victimization. Women were considered by slave traders to be less desirable cargo and were discarded in times of hardship, or if kept on board, had their children thrown overboard because they were too much of a

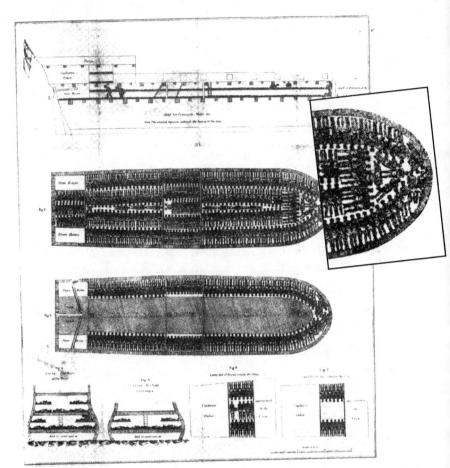

This famous diagram of a slave ship was actually a blueprint for stacking slaves for the trip from Africa. The inset shows a larger version of part of the ship, with slaves lying down below decks in a pattern that maximized the ship's capacity for its human cargo. There was no sanitation and little food. Abolitionists used images like this to publicize the cruelty that was inherent in the slave trade.

burden for their mothers.[3] Ocean transport of slaves involved over two thousand British and American ships and constituted such a large and profitable business that the British Parliament either could not or *would* not interfere with it.

Slavery and the Law

Although the death rate for Africans during the "middle passage" averaged about twenty percent, the profits for investors could be as high as one hundred fifty percent.[4] Lucrative economic connections among shippers, manufacturers, and mercantile interests on both coasts created a powerful lobby that overrode any moral or legal concerns.[5]

After the international slave trade was ended by federal law in 1808, domestic slave trade became highly profitable. With the South's increasing need for slaves due to the mechanization of the cotton industry, slave owners in the border states such as Virginia and Maryland found that by breeding slaves for sale, they could replace income lost due to the declining profits of tobacco growing. In 1826, slave owners in Virginia exported one hundred twenty thousand slaves at an average price of six hundred dollars. As an added bonus, slave-breeding owners learned that the continual presence of young children reduced the number of slaves who wanted to escape.[6]

When slaves were exported to the South, they were often driven in groups that walked hundreds of miles while chained together. According to one report from Shenandoah County, Virginia,

"*A drove of [black] human beings... has* just been driven past the door on their way to Tennessee and Georgia. They have been torn away from fathers, mothers, brothers, and sisters, and driven away without hope of ever again seeing them on this earth—bound hand to hand with iron cuffs and chains large enough to hold the strongest horse.... The number of slaves that passed was about forty.... The men were in irons and bound together in such a manner that they could not make the least resistance against any torture that their inhuman drivers might see fit to inflict upon them."[7]

Although some states enacted laws forbidding the domestic slave trade, both international and domestic laws were ignored and left unenforced during the antebellum period. As late as the 1850s, slaves were imported at New York City "with impunity," and blacks rarely had any success in suing for freedom on the basis of illegal importation.[8]

The legal status of slaves in America was so low that it is a wonder that they were even considered to be persons. Centuries earlier, Roman law had recognized slaves as things, not persons; but early American law did recognize slaves as persons—entities that could commit offenses against the law, and against whom offenses could be committed. Still, both state and federal laws cheapened the status of slaves by considering them to be property. It regarded them either as real estate attached to and encumbered with the land—a characteristic of early slave laws in the 1700s— or as chattel, property defined as personal and movable items such as tools or cattle—a characteristic of slave laws in the 1800s.[9]

In either case, the economic benefits of the owner/slave relationship took priority over humane, moral considerations. Thus was the institution of slavery reduced to a poker game in which the owner possessed all the chips. The relationship was not one of indenture in which the labor was owned as a payment for service rendered, but one of captivity in which the *person* was owned and deprived of freedom. Such slavery has been defined as "The complete subjection of one man to the will of another by force, the exercise of which was sanctioned by the statute law of the colonies and the subsequent states...."[10]

The slave in America could not testify in court against whites, could not be taught to read or write, had no right to contract, and no access to the civil or criminal courts.

> "He had no right to choose his own employment, to own property... to select his place of residence, to marry or to enjoy genuine family life, to become educated, to inherit property or to utilize the system of justice in any way."[11]

In short, the slave, throughout his life, was controlled by the law, but never protected by it.

Slavery and the Law

Before the ratification of the United States Constitution in 1788, the Articles of Confederation had left decisions regarding the control of slaves to each state. But the adoption of the Constitution raised questions about the power of federal law and the appropriate power of natural law. Antislavery advocates advanced the idea that natural or moral law—essentially the Golden Rule—inhered in all persons and institutions, was divinely ordained, and therefore took precedence over all sources of manmade law. They reasoned that even the newly adopted Constitution must be secondary to this 'natural' law. Therefore, the Constitution could not sanction slavery, because a 'higher court' had already rejected it as counterintuitive to the cause of liberty and justice for all.

Slave owners believed that natural law could not override the power of the Constitution, and that they had been given the nod of approval by those who framed the Constitution because those framers needed their support for ratification. The holders of "Slave Power," as the southern political bloc came to be called, gained strength and influence over national legislation. Their influence was seen in the 'three-fifths' rule— the decision of the Constitutional framers to allow slaves to be counted as three-fifths of a person for representational purposes.

A great irony arose because of the three-fifths rule. The practical politics of the Constitutional Convention overrode the dictates of conscience and reversed the attitudes of Northerners and Southerners regarding their perceptions of slaves. The northern representatives considered slaves as only pieces of property not to be counted as persons in the establishment of legislative representation; not surprisingly, the southern representatives saw them as human beings who deserved to be included in the resident population, thereby strengthening the southern lobby.

The three-fifths rule gave the southern states the political power they needed to control federal legislation and to elect pro-slavery presidents; yet this compromise supplanted the national fervor for human freedom that had been so important just a decade earlier, leaving the question of slavery to be settled by future generations.

An early symptom of this legal and moral compromise appeared during the first session of the new Congress, in which Quaker representatives brought petitions calling for the abolition of slavery. Said Congressman William Smith of South Carolina,

> "[We] made a compromise on both sides— we took each other, with our mutual bad habits and respective evils, for better, for worse; the Northern States adopted us with our slaves, and we adopted them with their Quakers."[12]

Thus the stage was set for the battle over freedom. By 1830, slavery had become so firmly institutionalized that Americans wrote it into their laws as a permanent condition, and the serious debate became not whether it should be abolished, but how it should be extended.[13] By then, lawmakers were working within a tradition of more than 150 years of slavery.

Early state laws in the South reflected the attitudes of a rigid class structure. A 1664 Maryland law stated that a white female who married a slave could be forced to serve her husband's owner for as long as her husband lived. A 1669 Virginia law exempted an owner from indictment for a felony if a slave died while being punished.

By 1680, laws had been enacted in Virginia to prevent slave insurrections. In 1692, a Virginia law provided for the legal capture of "outlying slaves" and the denial of trial by jury for slaves.[14] In 1705, Virginia had outlawed runaways and allowed that they could "be killed... by any person whatsoever, by such ways and means as he might think fit, without accusation or impeachment of any crime for so doing."[15]

Also in 1705, a Pennsylvania law legitimized the sale into slavery of a free black person who married a white person. By 1712, a South Carolina law prescribed the penalty of death for any slave who attempted to run away, or for any person encouraging such an attempt. If he was still alive after a second attempt, the slave was branded on the right cheek with the letter "R." In 1740, the same state decreed that "All Negroes...

Slavery and the Law

in this province, and all their issue and offspring born or to be born shall be... forever after absolute slaves...."

Before the 1803 purchase of the Louisiana Territory by the United States from France, the French treated slaves in the New Orleans area liberally and humanely. The new rulers changed that in 1806, imposing strict and punitive codes that removed legal status for slaves and authorized the breakup of slave families by sale. During the early 1800s in South Carolina, Georgia, Alabama, Mississippi, and North Carolina, a person inheriting a slave was prevented by law from freeing that slave except by special legislative permission, which was nearly impossible to acquire.[16]

One major concern of all southern states during the slavery era was what to do with free blacks. Several states enacted laws designed to rid themselves of free blacks because of the influence they had on slaves who came in contact with them. Because of their constant desire for freedom, slaves became obsessed with ideas of paid labor or of escape, and the presence of free blacks encouraged both. In the early 1800s, Virginia law forbade free blacks to enter the state and required all freed slaves to leave within one year or be seized and sold back into slavery. Arkansas, Georgia, Florida, and South Carolina enacted similar laws, and Alabama required black sailors entering port to be confined to their ships due to fear of the contagious effects their freedom would have on slaves there.[17]

Even in the North, discrimination against free blacks was common. In Cincinnati in 1829, some white citizens tried to enforce a local law that required blacks to post five hundred dollar bonds to ensure their good behavior. During the ensuing riot, several whites were killed. The resulting backlash in the community against blacks caused nearly one thousand of them to depart for Canada and form the Wilberforce settlement in Ontario.[18]

Southern states also enacted barbarous laws legitimizing physical punishment of slaves, often involving forms of torture. North Carolina legalized whipping and ear cropping, a practice in which one ear was nailed to a post for one hour, then cut off.[19] Such acts were considered by white southern courts to be only "moderate correction" techniques. Those who committed these acts were either acquitted of any charges, or if convicted, found that their sentences were unenforced.[20]

There was, however, an antislavery movement afloat in the country, and it was gaining force by the late 1700s. By 1804 the northern states of Vermont, New Hampshire, Massachusetts, Connecticut, Rhode Island, Pennsylvania, New Jersey, and New York had all either abolished slavery or adopted programs for gradual emancipation.[21]

New York lagged behind other northern states in freeing slaves because it had a greater vested interest in the institution of slavery. By the mid-1700s, New York had more slaves than any other colony north of Maryland; the health of its economy was therefore more dependent upon slave labor. Slaves made up fourteen percent of the state's population, many of them skilled craft workers who were "hired out" by owners to work away from their home bases and bring all wages earned back to their owners. This produced a substantial supplemental income for areas in the state—especially southern New York—that were not large producers of agricultural crops.[22]

In 1750, the number of slaves in New York state exceeded that of New England, New Jersey, and Pennsylvania combined. By 1810, one third of rural households in the state owned slaves.[23]

Control of slaves in New York, as a response to their abiding desire for freedom, was nearly as strict as it was in many southern states. In the 1680s slaves were forbidden by law to run away, and any slave found traveling north of Albany was subject to execution under suspicion of being enroute to Canada. Slaves were denied access to the courts, could not testify against whites, and were not allowed to assemble in groups larger than three.[24]

Following a slave rebellion in New York City in 1712, a new state law made 'manumission'—the freeing of a slave—difficult for slave owners to implement. Owners and executors of slave holders' estates were required to post a bond of two hundred pounds before freeing a slave, as a guarantee of non-rebellious behavior on the part of the future free black person. Although this requirement was rescinded in 1717, it was reinstituted in 1730 and remained in place until more liberal manumission laws were passed in 1785.

Even after New York State adopted a gradual abolition law in 1799, the rate of manumission of slaves was low and was applied most often to weed out poorer workers. New York's slave owners were reluctant to comply with the coming of abolition; the economic needs of businesses and the security needs of families overrode the moral considerations of manumission.[25]

In the early 1800s, with the advent of the Second Great Awakening as religious enthusiasm began to spread westward through New York, a moral wave inspired New York's legislators to move toward gradual emancipation. For all slaves born before 1799, bondage would end on July 4, 1827. Those born after 1799 might be required to serve a further period of indentured servitude until the age of twenty-eight if male, or twenty-five if female.[26]

To prevent New York's slave owners from reaping the value of their slave property before the 1827 date of emancipation arrived, the state enacted laws in 1801 and 1807 that forbade owners to take slaves outside of New York, where they might be sold into permanent slavery. Finally in 1828, lawmakers declared that "Every person born within this state, whether white or colored, is free; every person who shall hereafter be born in this state is free."[27]

Racial prejudices lingered during the nineteenth century, even as the abolition movement gained momentum. These prejudices reflected the chasm between the experience of free labor in the North and slave labor in the South.

Three

Free Labor versus Slave Labor and the Culture of the South

"**E**xtortion!" cried the slave as he labored for long hours without pay.

"Nonsense!" responded the slave owner, who saw servitude as a natural state for blacks, which he was generously enhancing with amenities such as shelter, food, and clothing.

This clash of ideas symbolized a cultural pattern of life conditioned by slave labor in which the worker had no input into decisions regarding working conditions, items produced, hours worked, benefits received, or even residential location.

The slave was ruled by a profitable alliance between southern Lords of the Lash and northern Lords of the Loom. Whereas southern landowners found it profitable to extort labor from slaves, northern textile merchants reaped profit through the purchase of inexpensive cotton. Even international trade supported slavery: In 1830, slave-produced cotton from the United States accounted for seventy-five percent of British imports, and ninety percent by 1860.[1]

A certain effect of slave labor was the dehumanization of the person. William Byrd II, a southern plantation owner, considered his physical and human property in united form as a "machine."

United States Senator Jefferson Davis—later to become the President of the Confederacy—said in a Senate speech delivered on

April 20, 1848, "Our slaves sustain the happiest relation that labor can sustain to capital. It is a paternal institution."[2]

Therein lay the problem that Davis and millions of other Southerners could not see: the slaves wanted *freedom*, not the supposedly glorious opportunity to be fathered through life by a superior-minded, paternalistic owner. As Unitarian clergyman William Ellery Channing wrote in his 1835 *Essay on Slavery*,

> "We have been told… that republican institutions are never so secure as when the laboring class is reduced to servitude…. A doctrine more irreverent, more fatal to republican institutions, was never fabricated in the councils of despotism."[3]

The dehumanized slave was a detriment not only to himself and his family, but to humanity and to social and physical progress as well. A British traveler noted:

> "Nothing can be conceived more inert than a slave; his unwilling labor is discovered by every step that he takes; he moves not if he can avoid it; if the eyes of the overseer be off him he sleeps; all is listless inactivity; all motion is evidently compulsory."[4]

When young slave Harriet Jacobs traveled from the United States to London as the caretaker of a child, she felt for the first time "the delightful consciousness of pure, unadulterated freedom…. I watched the tide of life that flowed through the streets, and found it a strange contrast to the stagnation in our Southern towns."[5]

Slaves resisted their situation by doing as little as possible unless they had the opportunity to express their own ingenious creativity in a setting that offered some hope of personal gain. Slave Jarm Logue—later to escape and gain fame as Jermain Wesley Loguen, a minister and Underground Railroad station master in Syracuse, New York—was on one occasion hired out by his owner to a neighbor who owned no slaves

Free Labor Versus Slave Labor

and was kind. His first task was to build his own log house. Loguen later wrote that the task made him feel dignified because "the growth of a young and unbroken spirit is rapid when the weight that crushed it is taken off."[6]

That "weight" would sometimes crush the socioeconomic development of entire areas. Kentucky, a state that was larger than the state of Ohio, had an 1800 population of just over one hundred eighty thousand—compared to the Ohio population of forty-five thousand. By 1840, Ohio had over one and a half million people to Kentucky's five hundred ninety-seven thousand. And Ohio boasted fifty-one thousand eight hundred students in its public schools compared to only thirty-five thousand five hundred students in the schools of all slave states combined.[7]

The suffocating effect of slave labor was reflected in Frederick Douglass' description of the Maryland slave village in which he lived as a boy:

"There were a few comfortable dwellings in it, but the place, as a whole, wore a dull, slovenly, enterprise-forsaken aspect.... St. Michael's had become a very unsaintly [and] unsightly place...."[8]

Different Views of Labor

Progress was stifled where slave labor produced a non-incentive-based economy that rejected the stimulation inherent in capitalism, manufacturing, and merchant profit. Slavery instilled a system of pessimism that had a cynical effect on the southern economy and its people. Both the *New York Tribune* and the *Cincinnati Gazette* published articles in 1857 and 1858 claiming that slavery retarded the development of the southern economy because, in the absence of capitalism, the South was not exploiting its rich natural resources.

The new Republican Party campaigned for northern votes, arguing the economic superiority of free labor. It was, party leaders reasoned, a more effective argument than moralizing against slavery.[9]

When We Get to Heaven

The important difference here is that in the South, labor was seen as degrading. In the North, it was honorable. The South developed a bipolar class division with no middle class, making it difficult for poor people—black or white—to improve their lots in life. Because one's status was inherited, there was little reason to hope for social or economic improvements. The individual spirit was stifled, thereby condemning southern society to a decadent and stagnant existence.

Northerners who wanted to move west declared that if slavery were allowed to extend into the new territories, they would refuse to migrate. This attracted attention to the fact that slave labor would influence the quality of life for everyone. They saw the choice between slavery and free labor to be one of national concern, because the lifestyles and attitudes of all inhabitants were conditioned thereby.

The culture that developed in the antebellum South was a *slave culture*, not just a culture with some slaves. The spirit and mood of society was polluted by the system of control that was required to maintain slave labor. The defenders of this system opposed reform and distrusted outsiders and, by design, any form of progressive thinking. The optimistic social experimentation that swept the North during this era could not penetrate the South's conservative and protective armor. The South clung to the anachronistic position of having a pre-capitalist economy dependent on capitalist markets.

Economic growth in the South reflected increases in quantity—but not quality or diversity—of products, thoughts, and lifestyles. While population and per-capita income rose in the North, they fell in the South, which also lagged behind northern states in the provision of public services such as education, literacy, and railroad construction. Children in the South were infected with social expectations that perpetuated the oppressive system. As Thomas Jefferson noted,

> "The parent storms, the child looks on... puts on the same airs [and] gives loose to the worst of passions; and thus nursed, educated, and daily exercised in tyranny,

Free Labor Versus Slave Labor

cannot but be stamped by it with odious peculiarities."[10]

Southern children learned to fear blacks. The constant need to repress slaves' freedoms was a considerable burden. It threatened the privileged lifestyle of slave-owning families and, perhaps, the children's own status as potential slave holders.[11]

The slaves felt deeply the impact of and irony within this intentionally discriminatory culture. Henry Bibb, a former slave, said after being emancipated,

> "Not tongue, nor pen ever has or can express the horrors of American Slavery.... The term slave to this day sounds with terror to my soul—a word too obnoxious to speak—a system too intolerable to be endured... [yet] almost the whole moral, political, and religious power of the nation [was] in favor of slavery and aggression, and against liberty and justice."[12]

Bibb and many thousands of other slaves sensed that the institution of slavery—and its great support in the United States—were contradictory to the intentions of those who had written the Declaration of Independence and the United States Constitution. For many slaves, the height of that contradiction—the source of greatest irony—was the celebration of Independence Day.

Even most abolitionists regarded the Fourth of July as a hypocritical celebration. At the early age of twenty-four, William Lloyd Garrison said,

> "For many years, the true friends of their country have witnessed the return of this great jubilee with a terror that no consolation could remove, with a grief that no flattery could assuage. They have seen that... Liberty has gone hand in hand with licentiousness [and that] slavery is a curse, debasing in its effect, cruel in its operation, fatal in its continuance."

When We Get to Heaven

William Lloyd Garrison was a lifelong activist who advocated immediate abolition.
From the portrait by Joe Flores. Courtesy of the National Abolition Hall of Fame & Museum

Garrison compared the grievances of the American colonies to those of the slave as being like "the stings of the wasp contrasted with the tortures of the inquisition.... Suppose that, by a miracle, the slaves should suddenly become white. Would you shut your eyes upon their sufferings, and calmly talk of constitutional limitation?"[13]

Ex-slave Frederick Douglass best stated the contradiction between American cultural philosophy and American cultural practice in an address to the Female Anti-slavery Society of Rochester, New York in 1852. He declined their invitation to speak on the Fourth of July because of his refusal to celebrate the day, but he agreed to speak on July fifth. His remarks so clearly depicted a great cultural irony that they deserve to be quoted at length:

Free Labor Versus Slave Labor

"What, am I to argue that it is wrong to make men brutes, to rob them of their liberty, to work them without wages, to keep them ignorant of their relations to their fellow men, to beat them with sticks, to flay their flesh with the lash, to load their limbs with irons, to hunt them with dogs, to sell them at auction, to sunder their families, to knock out their teeth, to burn their flesh, to starve them into obedience and submission to their master? **Must I argue that a system thus marked with blood, and stained with pollution, is wrong?**

"What, to the American slave, is your Fourth of July? I answer: a day that reveals to him, more than all other days in the year, the gross injustice and cruelty to which he is the constant victim. To him, your celebration is a sham; your boasted liberty, an unholy license; your national greatness, swelling vanity; your sounds of rejoicing are empty and heartless; your denunciation of tyrants, brass fronted impudence; your shouts of liberty and equality, hollow mockery; your prayers and hymns, your sermons and thanksgivings, with all your religious parade and solemnity, are, to him, mere bombast, fraud, deception, and hypocrisy—a thin veil to cover up crimes which would disgrace a nation of savages. **There is not a nation on the earth guilty of practices more shocking and bloody than are the people of the United States, at this very hour.**"[14]

[Bold-faced type indicates emphasis in Douglass' original document.]

These comments recognized the intelligence of all American slaves, whose ancestors had come from sophisticated cultures with complex economies. They had been skilled craftsmen, artists, technicians. They balanced socio-political systems and well-developed philosophical thought. These traditions they knew of through oral history, so they also knew that the supposed 'inevitability' of slavery had grown out of an institutional inertia maintained by people who were profiting from the status quo. They knew that their conditions as slaves were not determined by climate, geography, or genetics, but by decisions made by selfish people with power.

The tendency of most slave owners to rationalize southern slave culture rather than to abandon it made them tragic figures in a classic sense: Although they could have profited from other types of labor, they continued the social custom of slavery as a defense mechanism against self-indictment.

The slave owners' pattern of thought became a masterpiece of self-deception. It started in the early 1600s in Virginia, where Native Americans and poor whites were used as indentured servants. Colonists quickly learned that dark-skinned people were easier to control because they were more easily identified if they attempted escape.[15]

By the antebellum era in the 1800s, American whites in the South were convinced of the rightness of enslaving blacks, even though pre-Darwinian ideas regarding the climatic cause of differences in skin color evinced the equality of all races.[16]

To Southerners, slavery was deemed to be of benefit to both races because of natural differences, which made it both morally and legally right. Said journalist William Harper in his 1852 *Pro Slavery Argument*,

"Superior faculties and knowledge, and therefore…
superior powers, should control and dispose of those
who are inferior. It is as much in the order of nature
that men should enslave each other, as animals should
prey upon each other."[17]

Even President James Buchanan, in his 1860 message to Congress on the eve of the Civil War, claimed:

"Both the philanthropy and the self-interest of the
master have combined to produce [a] humane result
[for the slave]."[18]

Free Labor Versus Slave Labor

One of the most notable pro-slavery theorists was Virginia-born lawyer and journalist George Fitzhugh, whose aptly titled publication *Sociology for the South* posed the argument that conflict between labor and emerging wealth in the capitalistic North would lead to rigid class division worse than that produced by slavery in the South. Fitzhugh viewed liberalism as a form of paternalistic exploitation with implications for the lower class that were worse than slavery. He reasoned that the responsibilities of the southern plantation owner to the community—including the slaves—were socially healthier than the materialistic and competitive individualism of the predatory North.[19]

It is a credit to Fitzhugh that he did try to learn about the liberal attitudes of antislavery Northerners through extensive communication with abolitionist and Liberty Party advocate Gerrit Smith of Peterboro, NY.[20] The exchange of ideas, however, did not change Fitzhugh's mind, and he continued to support a variety of pseudo-scientific justifications for slavery.

The Pseudo-Science of Racism

Such justifications included, of course, the biological argument that blacks were racially inferior. In the 1840s Dr. Samuel Cartwright and Dr. Josiah Nott produced "research" that supposedly proved the racial inferiority of blacks based on brain size and differences in nervous, circulatory, and pulmonary systems. Some even advanced a faux-Biblical argument that noted that Hebrews had owned slaves; American slavery was therefor God's plan to expose heathen Africans to Christianity. Blacks were seen as inferior in their ability to learn, so emancipation was unnecessary because slaves could not be taught new occupations. Economically, it was impossible to send two or three million black people back to Africa; besides, they were now necessary to help run the American economy.[21]

An interesting contradiction regarding these racially based arguments was that while Southerners considered slavery to be biologically justified, under existing laws, a white father and a black mother could only produce a slave child. Clearly, the criterion for such a judgment was skin color, not race.[22]

Whatever the justifications and rationalizations, they worked to produce and maintain true believers in the cause of slavery. William Lloyd Garrison wrote as early as 1830,

> "It is morally impossible, I am convinced, for a slaveholder to reason correctly on the subject of slavery. His mind is warped by a thousand prejudices, and a thick cloud rests upon his mental vision. He was really taught to believe, that a certain class of beings were born for servitude [and claims to be a philanthropist for their good]. Does not every tyrant make the welfare of his subjects a plea for his conduct?"[23]

Abolitionist Lydia Maria Child consolidated such thought regarding slave holders by noting that,

> "In the habit of slavery are concentrated the strongest evils of human nature—vanity, pride, love of power, licentiousness, and indolence."[24]

Little wonder that the tyrannical control over supposedly inferior people devised by white male owners and overseers does remain in some quarters to this day.

Most slave owners did not perceive themselves to be tyrants, yet even a kind slave owner was no more than a benevolent despot. Thomas Jefferson was reputed to be a kind slave owner, yet thirty of his slaves escaped to the British army during the Revolutionary War. The reality for slave owners is that the spirit of the Revolution—even for Jefferson—succumbed quickly to racial prejudice and the thirst for wealth, with tyranny close behind.[25] A former slave lamented,

> "It is not true, that slave owners are respected for kindness to their slaves. The more tyrannical a master is, the more he will be favorably regarded by his neighboring planters..."[26]

Free Labor Versus Slave Labor

As an abolitionist, Lydia Maria Child supported moral suasion, but not political activity. *From the portrait by Joe Flores. Courtesy of the National Abolition Hall of Fame & Museum*

In his analysis of American society, visiting French scholar Alexis de Tocqueville noted that regarding slaves, Americans "have employed their despotism and their violence against the human mind" in creating a tyrannical system of control so complete that those who were ruled needed no physical restraints.[27]

In their 1830s study of American slavery, abolitionists Theodore Weld and Angelina Grimké wrote clearly about the mental state of slave owners that led to and justified their tyranny over subordinates. The slave owner, they argued, viewed slaves as things without feelings; hence he need not have feelings for them, and could treat them as "stock" or "merchandise." Such inhuman treatment of people gave the owner a heady sense of power that worsened the relationship further. Prejudice and power co-mingled to verify the notion that, as Weld put it,

> "men always hate those whom they oppress, and oppress those whom they hate, thus oppression and hatred mutually begetting and perpetuating each other——and we have a raging compound of fiery elements and disturbing forces, so stimulating and inflaming in the mind of the slaveholder against the slave, that it cannot but break forth upon him with desolating fury."

Weld's point was that "pride, scorn, lust of power, rage and revenge explode together upon the hapless victim" and produce similar attitudes in the slave, so having made "intelligence [into] property... its manager will have his match...."[28]

Tyrannical abuse of humanity became the slave owner's response to this match, which indelibly stamped the minds of slaves with images they could never forget. Solomon Northup, a kidnapped free black who became a slave for twelve years, said of his owner,

> "He could have stood unmoved and seen the tongues of his poor slaves torn out by the roots——he could have seen them burned to ashes over a slow fire, or gnawed to death by dogs, if it only brought him profit....
> He boasted of his cruelty...."

Northup would later recall that his owner had
> "... Daily witness of human suffering—listening to the agonizing screeches of the slave——beholding him writhing beneath the merciless lash... dying without attention, and buried without shroud or coffin—it cannot otherwise be expected than that [he] should become brutified and reckless of human life."[29]

Owners ruled their "troublesome property" with indifference, but they often grouped them along with luxury items as symbols of their economic strength. Rev. Phineas Smith of Centerville, New York, having

Free Labor Versus Slave Labor

lived for four years in the South, summed up the attitude of slave owners: "Avarice and cruelty are twin sisters; there is <u>less compassion</u> for working slaves at the south than for working oxen at the north."[30]

Support for this inhumanity was solidly established in the South. Colleges of medicine advertised for "sick Negroes" to purchase and use in labs for demonstration and educational purposes. Churches rationalized the slaves' subservience due to the lower cultural status of blacks.

Former slave Lewis Hayden pointed out the hypocrisy of some 'cultured' members of society:

> "I never saw anything in Kentucky, which made me suppose that ministers or professors of religion considered it any more wrong to separate families of slaves by sale than to separate any domestic animals.... I had more sympathy and kind advice in my efforts to get my freedom, from gamblers and such sort of men, than Christians."[31]

'Slave Power'

The purpose of legal institutions in general is to protect human rights. But in the South, government gave slave owners the power to wrest rights from the weak, thus attesting to the entrenched nature of what came to be called the "Slave Power."

The South owed its political power to the "three-fifths rule" made by the framers of the Constitution in 1787. It allowed southern states to count as part of their population for representational purposes three fifths of the slaves. Although slaves were not United States citizens, could not vote and did not have government representation, the three-fifths rule allowed southern states to stack state and national legislatures with extra representatives beyond those justified by its free citizen population.

The fact that two million slaves equaled one million two hundred thousand countable "free white citizens" gave the South an additional twenty representatives in Congress. This often weighted legislative decisions in favor of pro-slavery policies. The three-fifths rule gave national sanction to the institution of slavery, and gave southern states incentive to increase their numbers of slaves. Slave Power supported the vested financial and political interests of the South such that those who advocated change had to leave the South in order to achieve it. Yet when slave owners such as James G. Birney of Kentucky and the Grimké sisters of South Carolina defected to the North, they found racial prejudices there strong enough to support the southern intent to maintain slavery.[32]

Slave Power dominated Congress during the first half of the nineteenth century. Southern legislators held positions akin to feudal barons as they seated a succession of pro-slavery presidents, committee chairs, chief justices, and cabinet members. They managed decisions that prevented suppression of the domestic slave trade, allowed slavery to be spread into new territories, and brought new slave states into the Union.

This political power distorted established writings such as the Constitution and the Bible, both of which were misinterpreted to support slavery. Pro-slavery advocates denied blacks citizenship and suffrage on the basis of false biological theories. They suppressed knowledge and free speech, censored literature, defended immorality, and prohibited slaves' rights to petition and to seek trial by jury. They threatened citizens who aided slaves. They achieved a national commitment to slavery.[33]

These results could only have happened with passive assent of the North, where prejudice and racist feelings were still high. Many Northerners feared that emancipation would turn millions of blacks loose in the North. They worried about competition for jobs, the immorality of intermarriage, and the loss of political power and social status. Such attitudes would help spawn a backlash among some abolitionists in the formation of the Liberty Party and, later, the Republican Party, which supported the liberal policies of emancipation.[34] But for years before the Civil War, Slave Power held fast and controlled the lives of slaves.

The harshness of slave life makes it easy to understand why so many slaves became interested in the escape routes that led north to many points—including Peterboro, NY.

Four

Slave Life

"Massa sleeps in the feather bed,
Nigger sleeps on the floor;
When we get to heaven
There'll be no slaves no more."[1]

This slave poem aptly describes the influence of social structure on slave life. Forced to live on the barest of necessities, they hoped for a better life after death. Owners used religion as a convenient technique of social control because it taught slaves the value of meekness in the present life. God became an omnipresent overseer, promising eternal punishment for transgressions against what Christian slave owners established as rules of conduct.

Isolated from outside influences, the slave was subject to the ruler's whim. As Frederick Douglass described plantation life:
"The politician keeps away, because the [black] people have no votes, and the preacher keeps away because the people have no money.... The plantation resembles what the baronial domains were during the middle ages of Europe. Grim, cold and unapproachable by all genial influences from

[outside] communities, there it stands; full three hundred years behind the age in all that relates to humanity and morals."[2]

A House of Horrors

The slave's world was isolated in a house of horrors full of powers he could not control, people he did not like, work his owners did not appreciate, and mysteries he could neither understand nor solve. The legal status of slaves as chattel property ensured that they could not develop a prideful identity, but would exist in limbo somewhere between a proud cultural past and a degrading present. The slave could even lose his own sense of identity as a human. One Alabama slave, when asked how many were sold at an 1845 auction said, "There were five of us; myself and brother and three mules."[3]

Iron slave collars like this one weighed heavily on slaves' necks and shoulders, causing bleeding, infection, and permanent injuries. Slave owners often herded rows of slaves—dozens in a group, or "coffle"—for the long walk from the markets where they had bought them. They joined the collars together with chains up to 100 feet long that passed through the hasps of the padlock (lower left) attached to the collar. Some slaves had to walk hundreds of miles over several weeks in such coffles.

Photograph by Brian L. McDowell

Slave Life

Douglass also lamented,
> "Personality swallowed up in the sordid idea of property! Manhood lost in chattlehood!... I was only a slave; my wishes were nothing, and my happiness was the sport of my masters."[4]

The list of actions that were illegal for slaves was long—sometimes written in formal state law, sometimes locally established as plantation rules. Slaves could not gather in groups. A slave couldn't travel without a white person or a written pass, drink alcohol, ride a horse, own a dog, buy articles for resale, rent a living space, hire out his services, own or carry guns, or keep cattle or horses. Keeping chickens was usually allowed.

Slaves were allowed to marry, but their marriages did not have legal status, nor did they provide for the legitimacy of children or inheritance or transfer of property. Owners were free to divide slave families at will and to claim possession of anything their slaves 'owned'.[5]

During the antebellum period, one in three slave marriages was forcibly divided by sale, and one third of all children were separated from their slave parents.[6]

The effects of such policies on the personhood of slaves drew a remark from Douglass:
> "There is not beneath the sky an enemy to filial affection so destructive as slavery. It... made my brothers and sisters strangers to me; it converted the mother that bore me into a myth; it shrouded my father in mystery, and left me without an intelligible beginning in the world."[7]

These intense social handicaps delivered through the slave family structure were only worsened by those experienced during their daily work.

"It was work hard, get beatings, and half fed," said former slave Mary Reynolds. Sixteen-hour work days were common, usually from before sunrise until after sunset. And if the moon shone bright enough, work continued. Sickness or pregnancy mattered little, and "breaks" were nonexistent. Slaves ate their meals while working in the 'bite-and-work' technique. One slave owner complained that overworked women had a low reproduction rate.[8]

In the cotton fields, four hoeings were required during each crop cycle, as soil was moved to prevent weed growth and cotton plants were thinned to favor the strongest. Said former slave Solomon Northup,

> "If one falls behind or is a moment idle, he is whipped. In fact, the lash is flying from morning until night the whole daylong… an ordinary day's work is two hundred pounds [of cotton picked]. A slave who is accustomed to picking, is punished, if he or she brings in a less quantity than that."[9]

Ben Simpson, a Georgia slave, remarked,
> "Massa have a great, long whip played out of rawhide, and when one [of] the niggers fall behind or give out, he hit him with that whip. It take the hide every time he hit…."[10]

One former slave remembered her father's brutal murder at the hands of an owner who wanted to assert his authority:
> "My papa was strong. He never had a licking in his life. He helped the master, but one day the master says, 'Si. You got to have a whopping', and my poppa says, 'I never had a whopping and you can't whoop me.' And the master says, 'But I can kill you,' and he shot my papa down. My mama took him in the cabin and put him on a pallet. He died."[11]

Frederick Douglass noted that when the overseer rode by,
> "…the human cattle are in motion, wielding their

Slave Life

clumsy hoes; hurried on by no hope of reward, no sense of gratitude, no love of children, no prospect of bettering their condition; nothing save the dread and terror of the slave driver's lash. So goes one day, and so comes and goes another."[12]

This brutal system of labor merged with the 1793 introduction of the cotton gin to increase United States production of cotton by nine hundred twenty-one percent between 1819 and 1855, while the slave population rose by two hundred fifty-seven percent to nearly four million.[13]

Although the practice of slavery was visible to everyone, its horrors were kept closeted—even to Southerners. Artists' depictions of slave labor on nineteenth-century paper money in the South were efforts to publicly legitimize, glorify, and justify slavery. Slaves were generally depicted as well-treated, happy, healthy people working with no overseer. A ten-dollar note in 1853 from Farmers & Exchange Bank of Charleston, SC showed a well-dressed slave family working together, wearing shoes and smiling. A one-dollar note from Farmers Bank of Missouri in 1861 showed a happy slave resting at midday with his son.[14]

Those slaves on large plantations who worked in "The Big House" as house servants were often targets of abuse within the slave community because they usually worked less hard, were treated better, and were either envied or hated because they could become spies for masters.[15]

An artist's portrait of Solomon Northup. Northup was a free man who was captured and sold into slavery for twelve years.

With such demanding expectations regarding work, when did a slave rest? The only "vacation" time allotted to slaves by most owners revolved around Christmas, when the usual amount of time off was three days. "The other three hundred and sixty-two being days of weariness, and fear, and suffering, and unremitting labor," said Solomon Northup.[16]

Former slave Sara Gudger said,
> "I never knowed what it was to rest.... I had to do everything... till sometime I feels like my back surely break."[17]

When the work day did end, the slave continued to work—often after dark—at chores around his own home. Such chores included cutting wood, preparing meals, tending a small garden, grinding corn, and washing clothes. This was "free time," but it involved little of what might be called 'recreation'. When sleep finally came, it was seldom on a bed. "I never did sleep on a bedstead till after freedom. Just an old pile of rags in the corner," said Gudger.

Solomon Northup slept on "a plank twelve inches wide and ten feet long. My pillow was a stick of wood." Sometimes a "bed" might consist of corn shucks stuffed into any cloth container.[18] If little or poor rest were not enough to degrade one's lifestyle, the same qualities in food and clothing added to the burden.

Slaves often complained of being hungry, and what they did have to eat was the cheapest fare available. Regular rations doled out by owners included corn meal or potatoes, salt pork or bacon, and rare treats of molasses or meat. Owners expected slaves to grow their own vegetables during their spare time. Rations were often inadequate; owners used hunger as a control technique to yield good behavior. The quality of the food was poor; only North Carolina and Louisiana controlled rations by law, and neither required any meat.[19]

Clothing allotted to slaves was of the type intentionally designed to deliver a low self-opinion. "Negro cloth" was a coarse weave of wool or

Slave Life

cotton, usually ill-fitting, and not colorful. Each person received two shirts and one pair of pants per year, no socks, and perhaps one blanket. Clothes were seldom washed. Shoes, when available, were made of cowhide and fell apart quickly. One shabby pair per year did not serve the need.

As former slave Louisa Adams of North Carolina noted:
"My brother wore his shoes out, and had none at all thru winter. His feet cracked open and bled so bad you could track him by the blood."[20]

    Northup reported that one-half of a slave work crew of one hundred sixty-eight were naked as they worked.[21]

    The health of the slave family was always of concern to the owner, yet they often assumed that Africans and African Americans were physically stronger than whites and needed little medical attention. Children had scant parental contact after the age of four or five, as they were rushed into the work fields as early as possible. Some were used as scarecrows.

    Illness was common for slaves who, partly due to poor sanitary conditions, contracted respiratory diseases, bowel complaints, tetanus, yellow fever, malaria, and cholera. Owners rarely called physicians to attend to slaves because of the cost. Slave owner Robert H. Watkins of Alabama claimed that it was "cheaper to lose a few Negroes every year than to pay a physician" for their care. Besides, the owners often suspected their slaves of feigning illness in order to avoid work.

As nineteenth-century researcher Theodore Weld noted,
"If the medical skill of the overseer, or the slaves themselves, can contend successfully with the disease, they live, if not, they die. At all events, a physician is not to be called."

    Pseudo-medical treatments included good luck charms, brews, bloodletting, purging, and botanics, all of which contributed to the average life expectancy for a slave in 1850: twenty-one and one half years.[22]

Leaky Roofs and Hard Sleeping

The housing conditions for slaves also contributed to poor health. Houses were "cramped, crudely built, scantily furnished, unpainted, and dirty." With dirt floors, leaky roofs and drafty walls, they did not afford adequate protection from bad weather and insects.

Alabama slave Jenny Proctor recalled the harsh conditions in which she had lived:

> "We had old ragged huts made out of poles and some of the cracks chinked up with mud and moss and some of them wasn't. We didn't have no good beds, just scaffolds nailed up to the wall out of poles and the old ragged bedding thrown on them. That sure was hard sleeping, but even that feel good to our weary bones after them long hard days in the field."[23]

Slave quarters at an unknown location in the South. The spaces between the buildings were often occupied by chimneys that opened on both sides, offering an economical—and dangerous—source of warmth. Shacks like these were inexpensive to build and provided little comfort.

Photo courtesy of Norman K. Dann

Slave dwellings were often removed from the owner's sight, and a single hut rarely exceeded sixteen by eighteen feet—with an average of six persons per dwelling.[24]

In all, the appalling living conditions of slaves bothered owners little, and because they were sufficiently out of sight of the rest of the country's population, they attracted little attention and few calls for change except by the supposedly 'fanatical' and oft-ignored abolitionists.

Frederick Douglass summed up the situation well in 1855:
"[Slavery] can be indecent without shame, cruel without shuddering, and murderous without apprehension or fear of exposure."

Plantations, he said, are places where
"... public opinion... is not likely to be very effective in protecting the slave from cruelty.... That plantation is a little nation of its own.... The laws and institutions of the state... touch it nowhere.... The overseer is generally accuser, judge, jury, advocate and executioner."[25]

No wonder that the slaves took it upon themselves to resist their bondage. Historian David Brion Davis has noted the fundamental point that an internal contradiction in slavery was that although slaves were property, they were also human beings and could not be managed well.[26]

Black folklore symbolized their situation: "Br'er Rabbit" told tales in which the weak overpowered the strong. Music expressed the sorrow and depression of blacks at being relatively powerless and oppressed. They embraced religion because it promised a better future. Slaves clung to the optimistic hope that somehow they could overcome.

Abolitionist H. C. Wright noted in 1849 the conditions in which black slaves lived were unparalleled in their misery:
"There are no instances in the record of man, of more commendable forbearance, and suppression of revenge

and its murderous promptings, than are found among the oppressed of this republic."[27]

Methods of Resistance

Conscious accommodation, a technique of adjustment used by slaves who did not rebel, involved the adoption of the subservient 'Sambo' role in order to survive. This produced intense role conflicts in the slave's mind, with resulting identity problems. Each race was defined by the mutual struggle to maximize its power over the other. While the slave projected an identity that matched whatever his owner wanted, his internal self-knowledge contradicted that lie; so, in order to maintain personal balance, he recognized two sides of himself. As slave wisdom put it, "got one mind for the white folk to see, another for what I know is me."[28]

And what they knew about their desire for personal power, independence, and freedom drove them toward forms of resistance that varied from mild disobedience to violence or escape.

On the mild side, slaves justified the theft of owners' property because the owners had become rich as a result of stealing labor. Acquiring the products of their own labor was a common technique of resistance against a system that had deprived them of adequate living resources in the first place. It was viewed as a badge of status in the slave community.

Owners sometimes even expected and allowed small acts of theft as a part of their scheme of rewards, but they still perceived it as an immoral act committed by a lesser race. For the slave, theft was an economic and power issue, not a moral one. This was probably a fair perception; within a subculture in which one's possessions and life were not protected by any laws, one did not feel bound to respect others' laws.[29]

Another technique of resistance—one that revealed the level of desperation felt by many slaves—was self-mutilation. Because an injured or disabled slave could not work and would not be purchased by another owner, slaves sometimes disfigured themselves. In one case, a female slave who did not want to be sold away from her family chopped off her left hand with an axe. Having rendered herself unfit for sale, she was able to remain with her children.

More common were intentional bee stings, lacerations or cuts, or mild poisoning to produce sickness. In extreme cases, Slave mothers sometimes killed their own children to prevent their sale into slavery away from parents, and slave suicides as a technique of "escape" were not unknown.[30]

Probably the least obvious method of slave resistance was deception. Not only did slaves use deception regarding their own intelligence; they deceived owners regarding their health and abilities. When they worked, these dualistic tactics gave the slave at least some sense of having power over the owner—and pride in oneself. One "blind" slave magically regained his sight when freed. Some feigned deformed or useless limbs, and "sick" slaves deserved a day of rest. Former slave Harriet Jacobs justified the deceit:

> "Who can blame the slaves for being cunning? They are constantly compelled to resort to it. It is the only weapon of the weak and oppressed against the strength of their tyrants."[31]

Such deceit, however, bred mutual distrust and suspicion and, when punished, led to considerations of more violent resistance.[32]

Because the control level within the institution of slavery was high, armed rebellion against it from the inside was nearly impossible. When such conditions exist against oppressed people, it is not unusual for them to resort to forms of terror to oppose it.

For the slave, terrorist acts—called "rascality" by owners—took many forms. Slaves broke tools, degraded products, and injured or poisoned animal stock. They burned buildings, damaged fences, and defied owners' orders. They even injured, poisoned, or used other methods to kill their owners. Arson became so common in the South that some insurance companies refused to underwrite fire insurance in slave states.

Slaves who committed such acts were described by one owner as "turbulent, disobedient and impudent beyond endurance." These acts usually were committed by individuals as opposed to groups; doing it alone was less risky. Group efforts at violent resistance were more easily discovered, and they invariably brought forth swift and brutal punishments.

Most resistance involved spontaneous acts by specific individuals, not planned, coordinated efforts aimed at overthrowing the institution of slavery. Therefore, the specific individual causing the constant aggravation was singled out by the owner to become the target of severe punishment, the techniques of which were often horrific beyond belief.[33]

Five

Punishment of Resistance

"Are slaveholders dunces, or do they take all the rest of the world to be?" abolitionist Theodore Weld asked as he puzzled over the morality of slavery.

Weld noted that slaveholders were likely to say that they were "too humane... to stint the stomachs of their slaves, yet force their minds to starve.... Despots always insist that they are merciful."[1] The pervasive brutality of slavery is to be found in the loss of freedom through the exercise of unrestrained power.

As Angelina Grimké Weld put it,
"I may paint the agony of kindred torn from each other's arms, to meet no more in time; I may depict the inflictions of the blood-strained lash, but I cannot describe the daily, hourly, ceaseless torture, endured by the heart that is constantly trampled under the foot of despotic power."

As the Welds researched slavery, they described such despotic power as creating a viciously recurring cycle among punishment, depression, and pessimism. Angelina's sister Sarah wrote, " we [have] seen much oppression [and] truly we have felt its deadening influence." To them, the effects of oppression on *both* the victim and the aggressor extinguished attitudes of optimism towards the future.[2]

When We Get to Heaven

A fiery public speaker and a tireless researcher, Theodore Weld dedicated his early life to abolition.

It is a myth that the value of slaves kept owners from treating them harshly. Many owners seemed to feel that the only way to eradicate notions of freedom from the human mind was to bludgeon such notions to death—and that went for every slave, not just the disobedient ones. Said ex-slave Austin Steward,

> "No slave could possibly escape being punished. I care not how attentive they might be, nor how industrious—punished they certainly were.... Everywhere that Slavery exists, it is nothing but <u>slavery</u>.... Whips and chains are everywhere necessary to degrade and brutalize the slave in order to reduce him to the abject and humble state which Slavery requires."[3]

"There is a place down here," reported one former slave, "where the white folks... whip and hang the niggers.... They... hung and burnt people—killed 'em and destroyed 'em...."[4]

Punishment of Resistance

As such treatment went on, the general public did not seem to mind. In 1826, Moses Swain, president of the Gradual Emancipation Society of North Carolina, declared that "Generally, throughout the state, the African is an abused, monstrously outraged creature." Yet he noted the complacency of the public, saying, "Were all the miseries, the horrors of slavery, to burst at once into view, a peal of ... thunder could scarce strike greater alarm."[5] Public indifference to the plight of slaves was reflected in state law. In Virginia, only *three* crimes by white people were punishable by death: treason, first-degree murder, and arson. For slaves, *sixty-eight* crimes were so punishable.

In a North Carolina Supreme Court case, the court decided that an owner who shot a female slave who attempted to run during a whipping had violated no law. The South Carolina Supreme Court ruled that the criminal offense of assault and battery could not be committed against a slave, because the slave was not a person. Even Thomas Cobb, a lawyer writing in defense of slavery, had difficulty with the legal impotence of slaves in the face of an indifferent public and a cruel owner.[6]

Within this cultural setting, forms of punishment levied on slaves varied from those that hurt the mind to those that injured the body. Perhaps the most effective punishment rested in keeping the slave ignorant of his alternatives. Education of slaves in southern states was illegal, with a Kentucky grand jury stating that "school would enlighten the minds of those whose happiness obviously depends on their ignorance."

In his own narrative on slave life, former slave William Wells Brown declared, "The slaveholders generally do their utmost to perpetuate the mental darkness. The perpetuation of slavery depends on it." Such policy was based in owners' fears of what knowledgeable slaves would do, so the isolation and degradation of slaves was daily enforced through the constant surveillance and actions of the overseer.[7]

Most slaves lived on plantations that were too small to require an overseer and were, therefore, subject to the discipline of the owner, which was often more cruel than that of a hired overseer. Where plantations were large, mainly in the deep South, management of slaves was assigned to a "slave driver"——a trusted black slave—or a hired professional overseer.[8]

The Overseer

The overseer's main management tool was fear. In order to quell the slave's desire for freedom, overseers used rigid, harsh, and brutal punishment regularly to instill an attitude of unconditional submission. Probably the best way to feel the brutality of the overseer is through the narrative reports of slaves: "The requisite qualifications in an overseer," said Solomon Northup, " are utter heartlessness, brutality, and cruelty."

Austin Steward saw his overseer as
> "Pale with the passion, his eyes flashing and his stalwart frame trembling with rage, like some volcano, just ready to belch forth its fiery contents, and, in all its might and fury, spread death and destruction all around, he continues to wield the bloody lash on the broken flesh of the poor, pleading slave...."[9]

Former Alabama slave Jenny Proctor remembered,
> "We might-a done very well if the old driver hadn't been so mean, but the least little thing we do he beat us for it and put big chains round our ankles and make us work with them on till the blood be cut out all around our ankles."[10]

Frederick Douglass remembered his overseer's passion as well:
> "Reason is imprisoned here, and passions run wild. Like the fires of the prairie, once lighted, they are at the mercy of every wind, and must burn, till they have consumed all that is combustible within their remorseless grasp."[11]

Punishment of Resistance

The point that seems so unconscionable today is that the overseer's behavior was legal. When Arkansas slave owner R. A. Brunson sued his own hired overseer James Martin for killing a slave named Nath by means of brutal punishment, he lost.[12] Although overseers often carried with them weapons such as pistols and knives, the most devastating punishment was administered with a whip, a very visible and frightening instrument.

An illustration from *Uncle Tom's Cabin* shows Simon Legree frightening Tom. The threat of the whip was intense, and it drove slaves' fears of punishment and torture.

When We Get to Heaven

Escaped slave Jermain Loguen later became a station master on the Underground Railroad in Syracuse, NY.
Courtesy of Onondaga Historical Association

Punishment on the Plantation

Slaves were often whipped for seemingly minor infractions, or just for displeasing an owner or overseer. Former slave Mary Armstrong told of her owner whipping her nine-month-old sister to death because she was crying. Escaped slave Jermain Loguen reported being beaten to unconsciousness because he did not feed the pigs properly.[13]

Flogging with a cowhide whip on bare skin—usually the back—could leave open gashes as wide as a person's finger. Flogging sometimes involved hundreds of strikes, after which pain-inducing agents such as red pepper, salt, hot brine, or turpentine might be poured into the lacerated flesh. "Slaves were stripped of their clothing, faced against a tree or wall, tied down or made to hang from a beam, [and whipped]." The beatings provided owners and overseers with a vehicle to both chastise and

Punishment of Resistance

symbolically strip slaves of their personal pride and integrity while invoking terrifying images of the master's power." Solomon Northup said of the Epps plantation where he was a slave, "It is the literal, unvarnished truth that the crack of the lash and the shrieking of the slave can be heard from dark till bedtime on Epps' plantation...."[14]

Whippings were sometimes given in public to give examples to other slaves. Loguen watched as his mother was whipped for protesting the sale of his brother and sister.[15]

Other forms of punishment were used, but probably less frequently than whipping. Cruelty took the form of burning or branding one's flesh, cutting off ears, intentionally breaking limb bones, pulling out toe or fingernails, cutting the Achilles tendon, crushing hands or feet with a hammer, pouring hot tar on one's flesh and lighting it on fire, scalding with hot water, stabbing in nonlethal spots, and "cat hawling"—the dragging of a cat's claws across exposed flesh.[16]

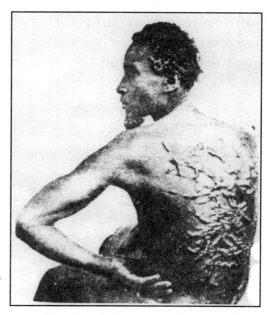

A slave's back, heavily scarred by the whip.

Extreme forms of physical mutilation were reserved for captured runaway slaves, and included chopping off feet or disfiguring legs, strapping or locking onto one's body chains, weights, or collars, or requiring work time which precluded rest.[17]

According to one former slave,

> "Nobody in the world ever got a chance to know as much misery as a slave that had escaped and been caught. So a whole lot of 'em went on north to Canada... because [they] thought it was the last gate before you got all the way *inside* of heaven."[18]

Novel forms of torture were devised that seemed to amuse sadistic owners. One owner drove nails through the sides of a wooden barrel, put a slave inside it, then rolled the barrel down a hill,[19] and Virginia slave owner Robert Carter devised the technique of lacerating the back with a stiff brush or curry comb "till he is well scraped," then "rub him down for several minutes [with dry hay], then salt him...."[20]

Such inhumane forms of punishment were common—even while owners built plantation churches and advocated Christianity as a ploy to keep slaves meek, obedient, and content.[21] Even the general public perceived such treatment of slaves to be legitimate. It is no wonder that slaves were prone to rebel.

Six

Rebellion and Escape

"A day...*will* come,... a terrible day of vengeance, when the master...will cry in vain for mercy," said former slave Solomon Northup. Having been a free man then a slave, he felt deeply a relentless drive for freedom.[1]

As early as 1835, slave owner-turned-abolitionist James G. Birney recognized freedom's motivating power by claiming slave insurrection to be "a brute force goaded into convulsive action, and animated by a love of liberty that no man can quench."[2]

Most slave owners could not see this; they believed that if they treated their slaves well, there would be no reason to revolt. When Louisiana owner William Dunbar caught his slaves plotting a revolt, he was perplexed, saying, "Of what avail is kindness and good usage when rewarded by such ingratitude[?]"[3]

The obvious question, of course, is why should people feel grateful for having been enslaved? Even the intellectual Thomas Jefferson tried to rationalize domestic racism by blaming King George III of England for inciting slave insurrections in the United States.[4] Jefferson established by this argument that he was insensitive to the formula about which he had written so clearly in the Declaration of Independence: Desire for freedom (democracy) plus tyrannical rule (slavery) equals revolt.

This type of widespread insensitivity to the plight of slaves united with other cultural forces such as economic depression, forcing owners to cut back on provisions for slaves or to break up families by selling them for income. At the same time, the spreading moral optimism of the religiously based Second Great Awakening, the expansion of opportunities fostered by increasing urbanization and industrialization, and the political debates over the morality of slavery spawned an increasingly visible abolition movement. The result was an increase in both the frequency and the severity of slave rebellions.[5]

That is not to say that slave revolts did not occur until the nineteenth century. Rebellions had occured from the inception of slavery, especially that brand of slavery practiced in the "New World." Compared to previous cultures of slavery, the form of slavery practiced in the Americas was the most degrading and brutal. It required the formation of "police states" on plantations to deal with the constant fear of slave uprisings. And away from the plantation, slaves found support from local free blacks and Native Americans.

The paranoia of southern slave owners seemed justified. Former Congressman Jabez E. Hammond proposed to New York State Anti-Slavery Society President Gerrit Smith in 1839 that blacks be trained in military schools in Canada and Mexico to lead slave revolts. Once trained, they could be sent into the slave states to do so. This plan was rejected by Anti-Slavery Society leaders William Lloyd Garrison, Smith, and Lewis and Arthur Tappan. But it did serve to kindle greater fears of insurrection in the South.[6]

The South developed a great fear of its own "peculiar institution." At the same time, there were increasing levels of abolitionist activity. There was John Brown's raid on Harpers Ferry. There was the advent of "free soilism" and the growth of the Republican Party. There were support networks for slave freedom throughout the country. All these things helped spark a greater frequency of slave revolts—and, of course, the war that would end slavery.

Rebellion and Escape

Boiling Point

As the South boiled, its inhabitants wrote of their fears. An article in 1861 from Jonesborough, Tennessee in *The Liberator* warned, "North Carolina, and perhaps the whole South is on the eve of a most sanguinary and desolating servile insurrection. That such a calamity is intelligently feared is certain; and its horrors may startle humanity at any moment."[7]

The advice of the white power structure in the South was: "Tighten restrictive laws, get rid of as many free Negroes as possible, keep the slaves ignorant, and your powder dry, hang the leaders, banish others, whip, crop, scourge scores, and above all keep it quiet, or, if you must talk, speak of the slaves 'contentedness and docility'!"[8]

In all, the fear of slave rebellion was well-based as they spanned the history of American slavery. On an individual level, slave rebellion was a common event. Slaves found many techniques of resistance and disobedience to protest their oppression. Rebellions that made news were those of large scale that resulted in personal injury or death, especially to whites. The history of slavery in the United States is marked by at least two hundred-fifty such events. It is likely that most revolts against owners went unreported because of the strain it would place on the reputations of the owners, fears that they would stimulate other revolts, or the scarcity of journalists.[9]

Well-planned slave rebellions were extremely difficult to carry out due to the high probability of exposure—especially from the inside. Two such efforts exposed by slaves more loyal to owners than to colleagues were the 1800 Gabriel plot in Virginia and the 1822 Denmark Vesey plot in South Carolina. In both cases, panicked whites rounded up and executed those blacks who had participated or had been implicated in the plot. But most rebellion plots were not large, and, when carried out, were quickly suppressed.

Even the famous Nat Turner rebellion of 1831 in Southampton County, VA near the North Carolina border lasted only a few days, and word of it did not spread far in the early aftermath.

If it seems a puzzle why slaves did not rebel in large numbers more frequently or with more success, one need only recall the power of slavery in the suppression of freedom. Yet a quick survey of the larger reported rebellions gives a sense of the determination of slaves in the face of obviously overwhelming odds to acquire freedom or die.

Table 1- Location of Major Slave Revolts

Year	Location	
1638	MA	
1663	VA	Plot exposed
1676	VA	
1687	VA	
1709	VA	
1710	VA	
1711	SC	
1712	NY	
1720	SC	
1722	VA	
1723	VA	
1723	MA	
1730	VA	
1730	SC	
1730	LA	
1739	SC	
1741	NY	
1763	LA	
1776	LA	
1795	LA	
1800	VA	Gabriel Plot exposed
1811	LA	
1822	SC	Vesey Plot exposed
1831	VA	Nat Turner rebeliion

Rebellion and Escape

It is interesting to note that these reported rebellions occurred nearly as often in states of the North as in those of the "Deep South," defined as those states south of Virginia. Simply put, wherever slavery existed, it created similar counteractions.[10]

The effects of slave rebellions were predictable. Owners' fears intensified as they armed themselves, their families, and their overseers, creating a police state that deprived everyone of liberty. Non-slave holders migrated northward to seek relief from paranoia and intermittent violence, and to take advantage of optimistic lifestyles and increasing economic success stimulated by the growth of industrialization. Other societal changes included an increased interest in the colonization of free blacks to rid the nation of people perceived as pests, and, very importantly, a spur to the development of the abolitionist movement, which aimed to create national awareness of the scourge of slavery.

The temporarily successful Nat Turner rebellion of 1831 spawned what would become a typical southern reaction. Fear spread as Southerners felt that if it could happen in Virginia, where 'happy darkies' and benevolent owners supposedly loved one another, then it could happen anywhere. Contagion trumped the dominant belief that all was well on the farm, and people realized that even seemingly trustworthy slaves were capable of hatred and rebellion. Whites' worst fears now held substance.

Insecurity grew and fed on rumor. Hysteria led to constant vigilance for one's life in a static, agrarian society where pessimism and despair governed social relationships. When Boston abolitionist William Lloyd Garrison was accused by the southern press of instigating the Nat Turner insurrection, he replied, "Ye accuse the pacific friends of emancipation of instigating the slaves to revolt.... The slaves need no incentive at our hands."[11] Indeed, they did not. And when open rebellion seemed futile—as it usually did—they resorted to a more secretive and individualistic style of rebellion: escape.

"Even with my good treatment," said former slave Martin Jackson, " I spent most of my time planning and thinking of running away."

When We Get to Heaven

The fact that even well-treated slaves wanted to escape testifies to the power of freedom. This seemed ludicrous to owners who felt that good treatment of inferior people was all that was needed to produce contentment. But what the owners ignored was that slaves *were* people—and not just troublesome property.

Frederick Douglass noted that kind and lenient masters encouraged more runaways than did more cruel ones, while his friend and colleague, black abolitionist Henry Highland Garnet, asked, " If [the slaves] were [content], how came it that thousands of them fled the house of bondage?"[13] Even in urban colonial Williamsburg, VA, where some slaves were educated in church-sponsored schools and most slaves were either house servants or skilled craft artisans, there were frequent escapes.[14]

Knowing that the desire for escape was always in the thoughts of even the most well-treated slaves makes one realize how tragic slaves must have felt during the nearly two hundred years before there was any free territory to flee into. With nowhere to run before the first northern states abolished slavery in the late 1700s, and with no 'Underground Railroad' network of aid to guide their flight, slaves must have felt completely trapped in a hostile world. But when the opportunity to achieve freedom did appear, many attempted escape.

The estimated number of escapees varies between fifty and one hundred thousand per year,[15] and that number does not include those who were not successful.

In fact, most "escapes" were in the form of truancy, as slaves became absent from their owner's plantation in order to visit nearby relatives or friends, go fishing, attend dances or religious meetings, get concessions from the owner, or just to get relief from constant labor. Slaves would sometimes establish camps in local swamps and stay away from the plantation for longer periods in what was called "lying out."

"Sometime a slave would run away and just live wild in the woods," said Jenny Proctor. Regarding Harriet Jacobs' hiding place in a swamp on her way north, Proctor added, "Even those large, venomous snakes

Rebellion and Escape

were less dreadful to my imagination than the white men in that community called 'civilized'."[16]

Owners might ignore such behavior with the knowledge that the temporary runaways would eventually return to their work.[17]

It is difficult to discern whether the ultimate decision to run for total freedom was painful or joyful. It was probably both, for it combined the loss of loved ones with the gain of personal freedom. There were, however, some events that gave impetus to escape attempts. The combination of the 1793 invention of the cotton gin and the 1808 ban on international slave trade forced slave owners in the deep South to look to the "breeder" states of Virginia and Maryland as sources of increased labor. The proximity of these states to free states encouraged slaves there to run north, as they faced the threat of being sold south or having their families split by sale.

In 1850, the strengthening of the federal Fugitive Slave Law reflected the worries of increasingly paranoid border-state slave owners, who were "looking around every corner for 'northern fanatics' spreading 'the evil influence of abolitionism'...."

The new, stricter rules were symptoms of a vicious cycle that encouraged escape: slave owners' worries about escape led to more oppression, which led to a greater desire to escape, which led to more worry about escape. The result was increasing paranoia to the point that even some whites were escaping to the North to avoid suspicion of aiding escaping blacks.[18]

In the event that a fugitive slave was captured—which happened frequently—he or she became a liability to the owner. There was a greater chance that he would try again, and that he would act as a mentor to other potential escapees. Captured runaways were often sold into the deep South at low prices; their reputation as "runners" decreased their market value.[19]

Following escape attempts, owners would work all their slaves harder in an effort to influence in-group solidarity against escapes. They even resorted to building private jails on the plantation to incarcerate captured fugitives. As an example of the problems slave owners faced, the Morville Plantation in Concordia Parish, LA had about one hundred slaves in the 1850s and experienced an average of three runaway incidents per month. Yet as discipline techniques there were intensified and capture-and-return techniques improved, the frequency of escapes increased.[20]

The reaction of many slave owners throughout the South was reflected in the comment of an Alabama owner who wanted "all [the fugitives] hung and the abolitionist with them." This owner knew that as the abolition movement spread and gained force, it supported a network of escape routes and "stations" that were safe houses for those slaves seeking freedom.

The people who were aiding runaways at these stations on the Underground Railroad knew that they were risking their fortunes and their stable social lifestyles for people whom they did not even know. Still, it was a cause they could not resist.

Of course, the slave risked something far greater as he followed "the drinking gourd" on the road north.[21]

Part II

On the Road

Seven

The Runaway Slave

"Why flees he thus? With burning shame
    My brow is flushed— for whence
Can draw forth a milder name,
    Than *outlawed innocence*?
Crime has not cankered deep his soul,
    Nor ill intent, his thought;
Yet, Christian's curses round him roll,
    His Brother loves him not.
Where goes he? Lo, the polar star
    A beacon shines before;
He leaves his native land afar,
    To tread a Monarch's shore.
He goes to take at Britain's hand
    The boon his home denies——
To drop his stigmatizing brand,
    And into manhood rise.
God's image! Freedom, favor, gain!
    These are inspiring food;
Behind, he leaves the whip and chain,
    Hate and brute servitude"[1]

                                          - Author unknown

Building the Underground Railroad

A lot of the myth and legend that surrounds images of the Underground Railroad is folklore and fantasy.[2] Still, it's clear that as a moral challenge to an unjust society, the Underground Railroad attracted the attention of the entire nation to the issue of racism. The railroad symbolized the best social principles of a developing nation: even those who were oppressed could be instilled with individual initiative, ambition, and optimism in the quest for freedom.

At an 1874 National Anti-Slavery Reunion in Chicago, Illinois Gov. John L. Beveridge noted in retrospect that, "The fleeing fugitive [was a] constant reminder of the inhumanity and barbarity of ... slavery." As a moral statement about an entire culture, the Underground Railroad stood as a symbol of natural law by directly challenging all man-made laws that contradicted it. Through their support of equality, the people who operated the Underground Railroad ushered in the antebellum era—along with the regional differences and strife that would be answered with conflict.

Boston abolitionist Franklin Benjamin Sanborn noted in 1863 that the essence of American social principles was found in the sagas of runaway slaves, and in the work of Underground Railroad workers like "conductor" Harriet Tubman and "station master" Gerrit Smith. Sanborn's colleague, Thomas Wentworth Higginson, agreed that the slaves' escape attempts showed more courage than did the actions of any other Americans.[3]

The Underground Railroad probably did more than any other institution to hasten the Civil War and the end of slavery. It stimulated a backlash in the passage of the 1850 Fugitive Slave Law, which allowed the capture of runaway slaves in the North. The law enraged Northerners, who decried the tyranny both of the slave owner and the U.S. Government. Surely no institution in the history of the United States has operated with such selfless dedication to its clients, fidelity among agents and clients, and harmony among its complicated and isolated units.

If the railroad's operation was invisible to the general public, its operators maintained a common purpose. It was highly successful.

The Runaway Slave

Although its managers knowingly faced heavy fines and imprisonment, they pursued their goals anyway, dedicated not to their own freedom or gain but to the freedom of people whom they did not know and probably would never meet. They sought no return, no publicity, no fame, as in anonymous work they dedicated their homes, wealth, reputation, family security, and lives to others.

And those others were so dedicated to the acquisition of freedom that death was no deterrent. When escaped slave Jermain Wesley Loguen spoke at an anti-fugitive slave law convention near his Underground Railroad station home in Syracuse, NY in 1850, he stated well the feelings of many slaves toward their owners:

"If to shoot down their assailants should forfeit their lives, such result was the least of the evil. They will have their liberties or die in their defence."[4]

Moses Roper noted in his *Narrative of My Escape from Slavery*:
"Tis liberty alone, that gives the flower of fleeting life
its luster and perfume;
And we are weeds without it."[5]

There were several ways for a slave to achieve freedom. Escape was only one; the others all left something to be desired. Manumission—the freeing of a slave by an owner—was possible, but highly unlikely, and few slaves spent their lives hoping for it. Emancipation seemed probable someday, but offered no hope for the present.

If the slave had a source of income, he might be able to purchase his freedom—if the owner did not raise his price at the last minute.

Suicides—the number of which probably about equaled the number of successful escapes—offered a bittersweet ending for many slaves who simply lost faith they would ever attain freedom on this earth.[6]

Escape appealed to the slave as the best option. It was a move that put him in complete control, usually for the first time in his life. As escapes occurred, they became news. Owners advertised in local newspapers seeking the return of their property, and northern newspapers reported both the frequency of runaway incidents and the increasing agitation of slave owners. This kept the abuses of slavery before the eyes of Northerners and fueled the development of the abolition movement and the Underground Railroad's network of physical and social links that aided fugitive slaves on the route to freedom. The railroad operated, according to Ohio Underground Railroad worker Isaac Beck, with

> "no regular organization, no constitution, no officers, no laws or agreement or rule except the 'Golden Rule,' and every man did what seemed right in his own eyes."[7]

Escapes increased when the Underground Railroad developed in the early nineteenth century, but they were always a part of American slavery. The earliest recorded escapes of slaves were in the early 1700s. In 1702, William Faussitt of Maryland sued Joseph Booth of Delaware for harboring " One Nigroe [run] away…," and the *Maryland Gazette* advertised on May 27, 1729 for the apprehension of a "Runaway… Negroe Fellow.…"

$150 REWARD.

RANAWAY from the subscriber, on the night of Monday the 11th July, a negro man named

TOM,

about 30 years of age, 5 feet 6 or 7 inches high; of dark color; heavy in the chest; several of his jaw teeth out; and upon his body are several old marks of the whip, one of them straight down the back. He took with him a quantity of clothing, and several hats.

A reward of $150 will be paid for his apprehension and security, if taken out of the State of Kentucky; $100 if taken in any county bordering on the Ohio river; $50 if taken in any of the interior counties except Fayette; or $20 if taken in the latter county.

july 12-84-tf   B. L. BOSTON.

The Kentucky owners of this runaway slave included his whipping scars in his description. They offered a higher bounty if he was captured outside the state.

The Runaway Slave

Hiding in Plain Sight

Prior to 1800, most Northerners did not favor runaway slaves, and many were apprehended and returned to their owners. But the increasing influence of Quakers, especially in Pennsylvania in the late 1700s and early 1800s, sparked the initial connections on what became known as the Underground Railroad.[8]

During the early 1800s, most slaves who escaped bondage showed little interest in going north, probably for several reasons. There were few 'free states' then, so slaves knew of no distant place where their freedom was guaranteed. Slaves had little knowledge of geography, and distances were huge—especially given primitive travel techniques.

The motives of early escapees were clearly more personal than political: they were, no doubt, far less aware of slavery as a major institution. They wanted either to avoid harsh treatment or to reunite families that had been split up by sale. Therefore, they did not go far. They established camps in nearly inaccessible places such as swamps, or became "hidden" in cities where large numbers of people made their identification difficult. According to analysis of newspaper ads, only five percent of slaves escaping from Tennessee plantations went north in 1815. By 1840, that figure had increased to twenty-five percent.[9]

In New York State, early runaway slaves in the 1700s had similar experiences, establishing small communities in swamps or forests. In the rural areas, they often obtained assistance at maintaining their freedom from local Native Americans.[10]

During the first two decades of the 1800s, as more northern states abolished slavery and links on the Underground Railroad improved in quality and increased in number, the northward trek became more attractive to escaping slaves. But what types of slaves were most likely to escape from the South?[11]

The 'typical' fugitive was a vigorous, energetic, intelligent male aged twenty to thirty-nine. He was optimistic and creative, with a need for high achievement and the ability to dedicate himself to a specific goal. With high levels of self-confidence and self-reliance, such a calculating and resourceful person could stay focused on his escape with such intensity as to overcome hardships while not losing courage. Of course, it helped if he was also light-skinned enough to be successful at deception.

Because flight was full of trials and threats, it revealed the escapee's inner self. Escape was a huge undertaking, and many slaves discovered strengths and weaknesses that had been hidden from them under the burden of slavery. A slave increased his chances if he was friendly and congenial, polite and pleasant. At the same time, he must have enough anger to win physical confrontations with those who might halt his progress.[12]

Selective Migration

This combination of traits in fugitive slaves who found freedom in the North produced a selective migration process, which one study suggests may have resulted by 1850 in a black working class in northern cities that held higher social status than did some members of the white population.[13] This is an interesting finding, because whereas racial bias against blacks remained relatively high in the North throughout the antebellum era, its effects did not prevent all blacks from succeeding there — although their lack of political freedom and equality sent many of them even farther north.

All escapees, however, were not young males. They did account for about eighty percent of those who escaped. They often found more opportunities for escape: owners hired them out, sent them on errands, or issued them passes for family visits off the plantation. Slave women were usually encumbered by children; still, they did attempt escape, usually in groups that proved to be a hindrance to efficient travel. Whereas men who escaped in groups usually went with friends, women, who left in groups nearly twice as often as did men, usually went with family members — including small children. The average 'group' of escapees was under three, because smaller groups had a greater chance of success.[14]

The Runaway Slave

Appearing first as a seal of the Society for the Abolition of Slavery in England in 1787, this wood-cut image of a slave pleading for his freedom became famous when it was added to a printing of John Greenleaf Whitter's poem, "Our Countrymen in Chains," in 1837. It came to be known as a symbol of the abolition movement in America.

Anyone who might feel that escapees had an easy time of it can read the narratives of Frederick Douglass or Jermain Loguen, or of many others, to lay that thought to rest. One fugitive who had just arrived in Pennsylvania was described as

"Weary, woe-begone and frightened. He had gone to
the limit and as he dropped into a chair… [he had a]
hopeless look on his face. Boots [worn] out at the sides,
soles and uppers held together by strings around the
feet, his clothes very scanty, scarcely enough to hide
his nakedness…"[15]

Such images prompted abolitionists to encourage and support escape attempts, and to devote their property to aiding runaways on the road.

Eight

Station Masters, Conductors, and Passengers

While Unitarian minister Samuel J. May, Jr. lived in Ohio in the early days of the Underground Railroad, he wondered at the inability of many whites throughout the state to understand the slaves' overwhelming hunger for freedom. "Their flight through the State is the best lecture—the pattering of their feet, that's the talk."[1]

Many Northerners were scared by Underground Railroad activity; it was illegal for slaves to escape, and illegal to aid them in that process. Yet those who did help escaping slaves became deeply committed to doing so. Most kept few records because of the threat of vengeance against them or the runaways. Daniel Gibbons, a station master in southern Pennsylvania, kept records of over one thousand escapees, including their real and assumed names. But when the Fugitive Slave Law was strengthened in 1850, he burned forty pages.[2]

It is estimated that there were as many as three thousand Underground Railroad 'operators' in northern states during the antebellum period, some of whom ran 'stations', or safe houses, for those on the run, and some of whom worked with "vigilance committees"—organizations formed in many locales to aid runaways with funds, connections, transportation, clothing, food or other needs.

The first such organization was formed in 1787 in Philadelphia, an early hub on routes north. Called the Free African Society, it helped runaways find homes and jobs, offered advice on legal rights, and provided legal services and connections on the route to Canada if desired. Vigilance committees, often staffed by free blacks, multiplied rapidly in northern states in the 1830s, and were successful in lobbying states to pass "personal liberty laws" in the 1840s to protect the rights of escaped slaves.

One technique these committees devised was to jail a fugitive on the accusation of a criminal offense so that he would have to remain in that free state, thereby protecting him from traveling slave catchers.[3]

In Massachusetts, it was common practice to imprison a fugitive for debt as a ruse to protect him from slave hunters, then free him when the threat had passed.[4] Monetary support for vigilance committees came mainly from local organizations and private individuals committed to the abolition of slavery. Jermain Loguen managed the Syracuse, NY-based Fugitive Aid Society, receiving aid from local donors, runaways who had found jobs, and women's organizations as far away as Britain. Wealthy sympathizers also supported committee activity. Gerrit Smith, landowner and abolitionist in central New York, was the president of the New York State Vigilance Committee in the early 1840s and contributed five hundred dollars (fifty thousand dollars by 2007 standards) to the New York State Vigilance Committee in 1848.[5]

Major supporters of Underground Railroad activity appeared throughout all northern states. In New York State, there were David Ruggles and the Tappan brothers in New York City; Henry Highland Garnet in Troy; Stephen Meyers in Albany; Jermain Wesley Loguen in Syracuse; James Caleb Jackson and Gerrit Smith in Peterboro; Frederick Douglass in Rochester; and William Wells Brown in Buffalo. All contributed massively of their time, money, and other resources to aid the flight of fugitive slaves.

The committed attitudes of such people were reflected in their advice to prospective runaway slaves. Henry Highland Garnet advised slaves that "voluntary submission" to the tyranny of owners was a sin. He encouraged them "to use every means both moral, intellectual, and physical,

Station Masters, Conductors, and Passengers

When the 1850 Anti-Fugitive Slave Law Convention in Cazenovia, NY drew more than 2,000 people, organizers moved from the Free Congregational Church to a nearby apple orchard on what is now Sullivan Street. This rare Daguerreotype shows Gerrit Smith (standing, center) and Frederick Douglass (seated to Smith's right) among the participants in the orchard.

Courtesy of the Madison County Historical Society

that promises success" at escaping from slavery, and "cease to toil for the heartless tyrants who give you no other reward but stripes and abuse." Garnet hoped they would stop work—or strike—for freedom. He realized that this would provoke owners to violent action, thus justifying a violent response by slaves. "There is not much hope of redemption without the shedding of blood," he said. He added this advice: "You had far better all die——die immediately, than live slaves and entail your wretchedness upon your posterity."[6]

Promptings for slaves to escape also came from Gerrit Smith, who at the 1850 Anti-Fugitive Slave Law Convention in Cazenovia, NY wrote the resolution that urged slaves "to plunder, burn, kill as you may have occasion to do to promote your escape." Referring to slave owners, he said, "Break their laws which forbid you to learn to read, break their laws which forbid you to escape, for the masters are but pirates and pirate victims can violate pirate laws freely." Frederick Douglass joined his friend in condemning slave owners, encouraging slaves to do anything necessary to escape. Smith added that slaves should be supplied not with Bibles, but with compasses and pistols.[7]

From Boston, the Garrisonian abolitionists were not quite as excited about encouraging slaves to escape because their focus was on abolition of slavery as a whole, not just on individual slaves. They viewed the resources spent on single slaves—either purchasing them as some abolitionists did in order to buy freedom for them, or aiding just a few escapees—as misspent, because those resources were not being aimed at the institution of slavery. Maria Chapman, a colleague of Garrison, called it a retail instead of a wholesale approach to the battle against slavery. Nevertheless, William Lloyd Garrison did issue in 1843 an address to "the slaves of the United States," urging them to run away and promising that they would find enough sympathetic Northerners to grease their paths to freedom.[8]

Station masters on the Underground Railroad were those property owners committed to donating their resources to benefit escaped slaves

Station Masters, Conductors, and Passengers

as they moved north toward free territory. Thousands of abolition-oriented people throughout the North joined the effort, building a network of informally connected destinations along a wide variety of routes.

A Railroad With Many Stops

These routes were always changing, as sympathizers on the route dropped out for such reasons as death, threats from neighbors, loss of interest, or moving of residence. The distance between stations was usually between ten and twelve miles, which was about as far as people or horses could travel at night without becoming too exhausted or attracting undue attention. Each station master would make a recommendation to the traveler as to which way to go and which person to contact next. Although a station was usually known by the name of the male owner, all persons living or working there helped in the process — and were sworn to secrecy concerning what or whom they had seen or heard.

What is remarkable, though, is how open the station masters were regarding their activities — in spite of the fact that there were slave catchers on the prowl in the North, and station masters often had reward prices on their heads. Some station masters even advertised their activities in local newspapers, encouraging runaways to seek them out. British abolitionist Joseph Sturge, on a visit to the United States, noted that "the slaves have... to contend with the honest and open-handed means which the abolitionists most righteously employ to facilitate the escape of slaves...."[9] Reference to a few of these station masters will help to illustrate their dedication to the cause of freedom for slaves.

Gerrit Smith aided hundreds of runaway slaves on their journeys to freedom. Levi Coffin, a Quaker who did most of his Underground Railroad station work in Ohio and Indiana, reported aiding over one hundred runaways per year for twenty years at his house in Newport, Indiana. Passengers on the road arrived at his residence — usually unannounced — every week. He carried on his operations openly, "without any fear of being molested," at a convergence of three different routes north.[10]

One of the more defiant and active station masters was Jermain Wesley Loguen in Syracuse, NY. Loguen escaped from slavery in Tennessee on Christmas Eve 1834, and, accompanied by one male friend—also a slave—engaged a long and difficult winter trek to Canada. Having started their travel posing as free blacks, the pair were advised by Underground Railroad contacts in the North to drop the ruse and admit to being escaped slaves. The reason was, if ironic, quite simple: transient runaways were more welcome than free blacks. Loguen's defiance showed best through his refusal to purchase his freedom, even in the face of credible capture threats from his former owner.

Loguen believed that freedom was a God-given human right, and therefore not for sale; if he purchased his freedom, he would be admitting to the legitimacy of slavery.

He participated in the "Jerry Rescue" in Syracuse in 1851—the forcible rescue of a captured former slave. The rescue was successful, and it actually dissuaded local law enforcement officials from pursuing other local runaways. This allowed Loguen to operate openly in aiding runaway slaves, even to the point of advertising his services.

One advertisement read, "We... hereby request that all fugitives from slavery coming this way, may be directed to [J.W. Loguen], and that all clothing or provisions contributed may be sent to his house...." He collected funds for his activities from Ladies' Aid Societies, which held penny collections, bazaars, bake sales, and benefit concerts. By the time of the Civil War, he had aided the escape of over fifteen hundred former slaves.[11]

Appreciation for his work appeared in several letters written in subsequent years by former slaves who had settled in the North.[12]

William Still was an active station master in Philadelphia, PA. Born a free black in New Jersey in 1821, he was self-educated. He became active on the executive committee of the Pennsylvania Anti-Slavery Society. Still recorded the stories of runaways for fourteen years, aiding an average of one hundred per year. He often received letters from them

Station Masters, Conductors, and Passengers

after they had settled in free territory.[13] He often worked with station master Thomas Garrett of Wilmington, DE, who over three decades aided an estimated twenty-five hundred runaways.

Also operating openly, Garrett was fined for his defiance, but kept his station open anyway. Garrison said of him, "What he promised he fulfilled... what he believed, he dared to proclaim on the housetop; what he ardently desired, and incessantly labored for, was the reign of universal freedom...."[14]

Such selfless dedication by thousands of station masters enabled many thousands of slaves to escape bondage for lives of freedom, but their journey north was anything but easy as they "followed the drinkin' gourd."

<u>The North Star</u>
Star of Freedom! Thou shalt be,
    A beacon to the fleeing slave!
How he fondly looks to thee,
    To snatch him from his living grave!
Through forest, rivers, swamps and plains,
    Beckoned by thy faithful ray;
From cruel tasks, and stripes and chains,
    On he wends his northward way! [15]

Although that "northward way" was supported by well-spaced safehouses on the Underground Railroad, it was also menaced by intangibles like bad weather, cloudy nights, slave catchers and their dogs, lack of food, medicine, clothing and shoes, and perhaps worst of all, racist Northerners who did not want their own status threatened by encroaching black 'foreigners' in need of jobs.

Much travel on "The Road" happened at night because of threats present during the day and because slaves often navigated by the North Star. During daylight hours runaways hid in barns, attics, swamps, and forests, thereby avoiding people both black and white, few of whom they were sure they could trust. Most slaves traveled alone or in small groups for long periods of time. Gerrit Smith wrote of two runaways who traveled at night "between two and three months" before reaching New York, and another report mentioned the passage of twenty-four men—probably also in small groups—through Mechanicsburg, Ohio in one night.[16]

Most slaves who succeeded in escape to the North started their journeys in the so-called "upper South," or "border states" along the Mason-Dixon line from which the route north was shorter and more well-defined than from states farther south. Those escaping from states in the deep south often ran toward the anonymity of New Orleans, or hid for long periods of time in inaccessible places like the Great Dismal Swamp on the border between Virginia and North Carolina.[18]

When they ran away from an owner, slaves usually traveled on foot for a number of reasons. First, they lacked money to pay for transportation by stage or train, and a black person traveling in public transport would attract unwanted attention. Also, it was safer to go on foot due to the ease of eluding captivity by hiding in places off of transportation routes like swamps and forests.

Runaways sometimes used horses—often stolen from an owner—but they found them difficult to maintain for need of food, water, and medical care. Slaves often escaped wearing scanty clothing and poor shoes, so long treks on foot could lead to serious problems of exposure and lacerated feet.[19] As they moved through rural hamlets, some whites would help them—especially if bribed by an item stolen from their owner's house "like a silver dish or spoons...." But many people along their route were unhappy to have runaway slaves nearby because they would "steal hogs, chickens and anything else they could get their hands on," according to a former slave.[20]

Few slaves were armed, according to William Still's records, and unless the slave was pursued by slave catchers, there were few cases of violence.[18] Although few slaves chose to flee via water transport, the

Station Masters, Conductors, and Passengers

chances for success may have been higher than on land because there was far less pursuit by slave catchers, there was less physical fatigue, and there was a prevalence of black workers on the ships and docks.[21]

Transportation by horse and wagon was relatively common, usually by someone associated with a station on the Underground Railroad. Station masters might disguise a runaway as a member of the opposite sex, or hide him under a load of hay or lumber or in false-bottom wagons. They might powder black faces with white talc, then transport their charges to the next station to the north. An ingenious undertaker named William Marks of Naples, NY transported fugitives to the next station in coffins. One Detroit station master kept his wagon disassembled for "repair," quickly reassembling it when needed, in order to avoid suspicion.[22] In a few cases, larger-than-usual groups of runaways would be led north by an Underground Railroad "conductor" who was familiar with safe routes, possible threats, and kind station masters. One such renowned conductor was Harriet Tubman.

Conductor Tubman

The number of trips that Tubman made into slave territory after her initial escape, and the number of slaves she led to freedom are open to question. What is known is that she returned several times to conduct slaves — many of whom she knew from her slavery days — along routes north familiar to her. She conducted them north in groups — once reporting a group as large as nine — under circumstances which, to her, seemed to offer the greatest chance of success.

Tubman usually traveled in winter when nights were long and people stayed inside their homes, thus ensuring that she could find the people she needed to contact, and that she would have maximum travel time at night. Winter was also the time when southern slave traders came to the border states in search of new stock to buy for work on the cotton plantations. Virginia and Maryland planters in need of cash would sell slaves into the deep south, thereby increasing the motivation to escape to the North.[23]

When We Get to Heaven

Like other conductors, Tubman was a practical person who preferred to expend her efforts toward individually targeted goals that could lead to quick, visible success. She risked her own hard-won freedom, and perhaps her life, with every trip. The most intense peril she and all fugitive slaves faced was the prospect of being caught by slave catchers who traveled into the North, or by patrollers who watched the southern roadways for suspicious blacks. The slaves warned themselves in rhyme:

> "Run nigger, run.
>   The paddyroll get you!
> Run nigger, run
>   The paddyroll come.
> Watch nigger, watch,
>   The paddyroll trick you!
> Watch nigger, watch
>   He got a big gun."[24]

Worried plantation owners supplied and paid bands of young white men to police areas between plantations for blacks who were suspected of escaping or becoming involved in other mischief, such as stealing or attempting to sabotage plantation activities. Patrol members had by "general consent" the authority to capture and punish any black person off the plantation, often to an abusive extent.

Patrollers were often intoxicated with alcohol, or power, or both, and perceived their work as a macho sport, administering excessive punishment for minor or assumed offences. Such patrols were necessary in spite of the fact that slave owners tried to instill in their slaves great fears regarding running away. In fact, the goal of the patrols was to instill fear in potential escapees. In the words of one former slave, "Jim Williams was a patroller, and how he did like to catch a nigger off the farm without a permit so he could whip him."[25]

All white men in South Carolina were required to serve on slave patrols, and were authorized by the state to maim or kill any resistors.

Station Masters, Conductors, and Passengers

Patrols provided some psychological comfort for slave owners. They became a form of racial police assigned to an organized "beat" or territory in which they were required to conduct surprise monthly inspections of slave quarters in order to flush out potential runaways. Serving on a patrol was considered to be a status symbol for many white males who, after the Civil War, transformed themselves into the Ku Klux Klan.[26]

Slaves were warned about harsh, cold weather in the North, isolation from family, being mangled by pursuit dogs, poor treatment by abolitionists and prejudiced Northerners, starvation, sickness, and the certainty of severe punishment if caught. North and South Carolina enacted laws permitting any person to kill a slave for running away, or for aiding an escaping slave. Several southern states repelled free black residents and travelers with the threat that they would be captured and sold into slavery.[27]

While travelling north, runaways also faced the threat of fraudulent station masters who were really slave catchers. George Walls of Oxford, PA would lure blacks to his house, then notify owners of when and where to capture them.

On the other side, some fraudulent blacks would decoy philanthropic white Northerners into believing that they were runaway slaves so that they could collect money for their 'escape'. The distrust flowing in both directions was common in the antebellum period, but by far the greater share of it was harbored by the runaways, many of whom reported feelings of not being able to trust anyone in the North—even free blacks.[28]

Saratoga, NY free black Solomon Northup, a violin player, experienced a classic case of fraudulent solicitation when he was approached by two white men who claimed they were operating a circus in Washington, D.C. and were looking for talent. Solomon was hired and taken to Washington, where he was paid, boarded and fed. He said of his captors,

> "They were... extremely kind.... I gave them my confidence without reserve, and would freely have trusted them to almost any extent. Their constant

> conversation and manner towards me... indicated that they were friends indeed, sincerely solicitous for my welfare."

Solomon was then sold into slavery. When he was freed twelve years later, he indicated that other free blacks were similarly treated.[29]

Bounty hunters stalked northern cities, capturing both runaway slaves and free blacks either for return to owners for a reward, or to sell into slavery. The New York City Vigilance Committee reported in 1838 that such kidnappings were occurring "almost daily," and they were common in the border city of Philadelphia. One gang of slave catchers that operated in southeastern Pennsylvania was called the "Gap Gang." Its members often sold kidnapped black people at slave auctions.[30]

The business of slave catching boomed after 1850, with some bounty hunters bragging that if they had a description of an escapee, they would find a Negro to fit it.[31]

When runaway slaves were discovered by slave catchers, their resistance was often futile because of their lack of weapons for defense. The capture of runaways was common and could occur anywhere in the North; the price paid for capture and return increased the farther north the capture was made.

Fights were common, often resulting in debilitating injuries. Jermain Loguen was clubbed on the head during one of the two fights he had with slave catchers during his successful escape attempt, but the violence could also turn against the pursuers. Slave owner Edward Gorsuch was killed in his attempt to capture his escaped slave at Christiana, Pennsylvania.[32] Usually, though, the violence hurt the slave more—even to the point of death.

Owners advertised rewards for runaway slaves "dead or alive," indicating their intense irritation over the fact that one of their own had attempted to gain freedom. Some owners even made gruesome public displays of body parts—usually heads—of the runaways who had been killed during their capture.[33]

Station Masters, Conductors, and Passengers

One of the most tragic examples of runaway slaves' reaction to capture is the story of Margaret Garner who, with her four children, ran away from her owner James Marshall of Boone County, Kentucky on January 27, 1856. When caught in a house in Cincinnati, Ohio by slave catchers, she killed her three-year-old daughter and wounded two of her sons in an attempt to kill them with a butcher knife rather than see them returned to slavery. According to one researcher, "The way Margaret Garner's little girl died embarrassed the South and disturbed the North more than a hundred arguments of antislavery philosophers."[34]

Those runaway slaves who did achieve freedom told harrowing tales of beating the bad weather, illness, hunger, the threat of betrayal, slave catchers, and hunting dogs. They waded streams and rivers to avoid detection by scent, or rubbed the foul-smelling herb asafetida on their shoes or feet. One enterprising conductor on the Underground Railroad, Theron Trowbridge of Denmark, Iowa, invented what he called "Hush Puppies"——corn bread containing strychnine which was fed to dogs used to track runaway slaves.[35] They hid in barns, attics, cellars, swamps and woods, always in fear that they would be detected and sent back to slavery and certain punishment.[36] And in the face of capture, some threatened or committed suicide.[37]

In some of the more creative escapes, slaves disguised themselves as legitimate travellers or boxed themselves and were shipped north. But such occurrences were rare compared to those who found themselves subjected to plantation law, state law, or national law—and failed in their attempts.[38]

Nine

Fugitive Slave Laws and Northern Prejudice

"It is the monster iniquity of the present age," Boston antislavery preacher Charles Beecher said in 1851, "and will stand forever on the page of history, as the vilest monument of infamy of the nineteenth century.... Nations afar off pause... to ask what will those Christians do next."

Beecher was talking about fugitive slave laws that sanctioned the capture and return to slavery of those who had successfully escaped.[1] There were both state and federal laws about runaway slaves, yet slave owners were never fully satisfied. They knew that legislation could not change the intent to escape the horror of being a slave.

All southern states enacted laws regarding runaway slaves. The laws covered the aspects of "identifying, capturing, jailing, advertising, returning, and selling" them. In 1659, Maryland legislators enacted laws regarding the treatment and return of runaways. North Carolina followed in 1699. By 1715, North Carolina law reimbursed the expenses of slave capturers; in 1741, the state's leaders strengthened that law because the escape problem was getting worse. They added a fine on anyone who aided a slave's escape, requiring that person to serve the slave's owner for five years if he could not pay the fine.

In 1753, North Carolina legally established patrollers in each county to apprehend runaways and to search slave quarters for weapons, offering tax incentives to those who would serve as patrollers. This patrol law was strengthened in 1794, 1802, and 1830. Also in 1830, the radical abolitionist book *Walkers' Appeal* was banned in North Carolina. By 1792, that state had sanctioned the death penalty to anyone who had helped to transport a slave out of the state.[2]

One problem for southern states was the difficulty in distinguishing slaves from free black people. While several southern states required registration of free blacks and others even required them to have white guardians, all required them to carry passes or certificates of freedom.[3]

In 1793, the federal government addressed the issue of runaway slaves in accordance with allowances within the United States Constitution by enacting a Fugitive Slave Law that read,

> "No Person held to Service or Labour in one State, under the Laws thereof, escaping into another, shall in Consequence of any law or Regulation therein, be discharged from such Service or Labour, but shall be delivered up on Claim of the Party to whom such Service or Labor may be due."[4]

Under this law, a slave owner needed only to claim his human property orally and could use professional bounty hunters to capture escaped slaves. A local magistrate had authority to decide the case, often basing a decision on bribery or racial prejudice.

Anyone aiding an escaped slave could be fined five hundred dollars; any northern person had legal authority to stop any black person and demand to see a pass, certificate of freedom, or emancipation papers.[5]

Reaction was not identical in all northern states. In Ohio, although the transplanted antislavery tradition of New England ran high, an 1839 law affirmed Ohio's intent to uphold the Constitution by returning fugitive slaves to their state of origin and enforcing a fine and jail term for those who aided fugitives. But in New York, abolitionist and Liberty Party co-founder Alvan Stewart dedicated Liberty Party political efforts to the

Fugitive Slave Laws and Northern Prejudice

repeal of the 1793 federal law, saying, "This is the Law of slavery on our soil. Let us be candid. This is more cruel, meaner, [and] infinitely more degrading than running men and women down in the woods of Africa" because they can call on the law to help them do it.[6]

The constitutionality of both the 1793 federal law and subsequent state laws dealing with the capture and return of fugitive slaves were addressed by the U.S. Supreme Court case of Prigg v Pennsylvania in 1842. Edward Prigg, an agent for a southern slave holder, captured his owner's runaway slave in Pennsylvania and applied through that state for 'certificates of removal" under the 1793 Fugitive Slave Law to return Margaret Morgan and her two children to Maryland. The state had higher standards for identification of runaway slaves than federal law dicatated, however, and state authorities refused Prigg's request. When he left the state with the three slaves without state consent, he was tried and convicted under a state kidnapping law.

The Pennsylvania Supreme Court upheld his conviction for illegal kidnapping. His appeal to the U.S. Supreme Court, however, went differently. The U.S. Supreme Court voted 8-1 to reverse Prigg's conviction, upholding the 1793 Fugitive Slave Law, which allowed an owner to retrieve his own escaped property. The decision concluded that state law could not restrain an owner from retrieving his slave, but added that state authorities were not required to assist in the seizure process.

This rendered the previously mentioned 1839 Ohio law unconstitutional on the grounds that the 1793 federal law could be enforced only by federal authorities, so states had no jurisdiction on fugitive slave cases. Because state authorities could no longer participate in the capture and return of fugitive slaves, legislators in southern states angrily demanded a strengthening of the 1793 law. The result was the Fugitive Slave Law of 1850, which required Northerners to help recover escaped slaves.[7]

By 1850, people in the North were bracing for conflict with people in the South over the issue of slavery. Developments in the North that angered the South included an increase in the number and the aggressiveness of the demands of abolitionists, an increase in the number of antislavery newspapers, the decision of the U.S. Supreme Court in the Prigg case, improvements in transportation and an expansion of connections on the Underground Railroad, allowance of trial by jury for escaped slaves, and the increasing tendency of wealthy abolitionists to buy the freedom of slaves. As a result, on January 4, 1850, Senator James Mason of Virginia introduced, as a part of the Compromise of 1850, what came to be called the Fugitive Slave Law of 1850. The bill passed in the Senate on August 26, and in the House on September 12, and was signed into law by President Millard Fillmore on September 18.[8]

The provisions of this law put the acquisition and return of fugitive slaves in the hands of federal authorities, thereby avoiding the unconstitutional involvement of state officials. The law empowered a slave owner to seize his human property anywhere in the country based on his own oral testimony and without a warrant. Northern citizens could be deputized—without their consent—by a U.S. marshal who was pursuing a fugitive slave. If they refused to assist in the capture, they could be fined up to one thousand dollars and imprisoned up to six months. They were also liable for civil damages of up to one thousand dollars for each slave lost. Federal marshals were rewarded financially for the return of each captured slave, thus encouraging their support of the slave owners.[9]

Northern reaction to this 1850 federal law set off a mini-revolution, as people viewed the government policy as a despotic and unnecessary effect of the "Slave Power" that had dominated national politics for decades. It infuriated Northerners by placing economics above human rights, property over people. In time, it would backfire against the South; it did not stem the tide of runaways, but instead stimulated the growth of antislavery attitudes. Abolitionists called it "the bloodhound bill" or "the infamous law." They publicly refused to obey it and undertook several rescues of captured slaves in northern cities to dramatize their opposition.

The law even terrorized free blacks in the North by threatening them with capture by overzealous slave catchers for sale into slavery.

Fugitive Slave Laws and Northern Prejudice

Frederick Douglass noted,
"It was intended to put thorns under feet already bleeding; to crush a people already bowed down; to enslave a people already but half free; in a word, it was intended to discourage, dishearten, and drive the free colored people out of the country."

Northern state antislavery organizations responded in like fashion, with Massachusetts officials declaring that the law should be "resisted, disobeyed, and trampled under foot at all hazards," and Rhode Island legislators adding,
"Every peaceful instrumentality shall be energetically used to make the slave hunters aware that the atmosphere of the free states is unfavorable for their health, so that they shall be exceedingly glad to go home."[10]

The effect of the Fugitive Slave Law of 1850 on the actual return of runaways was minimal, resulting in the capture and return to slavery of about eighteen slaves per year, but the reaction of southern slave owners to northern opposition to the law was malevolent. Rewards were offered for information leading to those who had aided an escape, with punishment for the helper being branded on the hand with "SS" for Slave Stealer. When Underground Railroad ship captain Jonathan Walker was so branded in 1844, abolitionist poet John Greenleaf Whittier wrote about him:
"Then lift that manly right hand, bold
    Plowman of the wave
Its branded palm shall prophesy
    'Salvation to the Slave.' "

Also as part of the brutality of reactionary slave owners, returned runaways might be branded on the face with an "R" to show the stigma of being a runner, or punished more severely than others for future infractions of plantation rules.[11]

When We Get to Heaven

While it is reassuring in the light of human rights to know that both the 1793 and the 1850 Fugitive Slave Laws were repealed on June 28, 1864, it is disheartening to consider the prejudice shown by Northerners toward black people both before and after the Civil War.[12]

Slaves who left the South ran from everything familiar into a mythical world of which they knew little more than its irresistible offer of freedom. Their naïve view of "Heaven"—the North—spawned idealized dreams of a new homeland free of prejudice and discrimination, sometimes expressed in spirituals:

"Dark and thorny is the pathway,
   Where the pilgrim makes his way;
But beyond this vale of sorrow,
   Lie the fields of endless days."[13]

Once in the North, runaway slaves quickly learned that, although slavery by 1850 had become a sectional issue, the racist attitudes that successfully sustained it were found throughout the country. With racial discrimination rampant and slave catchers on their heels, blacks arriving in the North found it to be a disappointing place. Jermain Loguen stated the case clearly when, as a twenty-one-year-old escapee, he stood at the edge of Lake Ontario poised for a life of freedom.

"There I stood,... the tempest [of winter] howling over my head, and my toes touching the snow beneath my worn-out shoes... knowing nobody, and nobody knowing me or noticing me ... I stood there the personification of helpless courage.... Was it for this that I left sweet [southern] skies and a mother's love?... I had freedom, but nature and man were against me."[14]

Perhaps the harshest reality that the newly free former slave had to face was the crushing sense of loneliness. Loved ones left behind in their dash to freedom weighed heavily on their hearts. Harriet Tubman re-

Fugitive Slave Laws and Northern Prejudice

turned to the slave states several times to rescue members of her family. Contemporary song writers Kim and Reggie Harris have expressed the slaves' plight beautifully:

"And I miss you now, when the snow falls around me.
The chains that I used to wear are
    wrapped around my heart
And I need you now, for my burden is so heavy.
Without you here, heaven is less than fair."

The hypocritical double standard of expectations in northern society was unfair as well. Optimism, self-confidence, equal opportunity, social mobility, a growing middle class, and spreading democratic institutions were what northern natives expected for themselves, but they withheld them from blacks. Frederick Douglass noted the irony:

"People will not allow that we have a head to think and a heart to feel and a soul to aspire. You degrade us and then ask why we are so degraded—you shut our mouths and then ask why we don't speak—you close your colleges and schools against us and then ask why we don't know more."[15]

Northern attitudes toward black people—especially runaway slaves— were often hostile. Poor whites were on the lookout for blacks without papers certifying their freedom because of the windfall profits that came with capture. In 1832, a northern state resident upon returning a runaway slave to Virginia would receive a fifty dollar reward plus expenses of twenty cents per mile traveled. Many Northerners considered runaways to be a nuisance because of their tendency to steal provisions for their journey such as clothing, weapons, vegetables, chickens, or other farm animals for food.[16]

The city of Philadelphia, situated in southeastern Pennsylvania near the border of slave states, was considered to be a haven for runaway slaves in the 1830s. It was home to black abolitionists James Forten and

When We Get to Heaven

Robert Purvis, who supported a protective network of black informants that kept runaways aware of dangers such as the presence and movements of slave catchers. Forten and Purvis worked through The Pennsylvania Society for the Promotion of the Abolition of Slavery, one of the first antislavery organizations in the country, which had its headquarters there.

By 1830 only twelve slaves lived in Philadelphia, down from six thousand in 1750. Economic opportunity and social mobility were available to blacks. Even so, there was much racial prejudice against blacks as racial aspersion appeared in print in newspapers:

> "Who... is the most *protected*, the most *insolent*, the most *assuming*, the most *depraved* the most *dangerous* of our population? We answer the Negro;... The Thick-Lipped, Wolley-Headed, Skunk-Smelling, combination of the MONKEY AND THE DEVIL."[17]

As the black population of Philadelphia grew during the antebellum period, it fueled racial prejudice. On January 3, 1861, a petition signed by eleven thousand Pennsylvanians—mostly persons from the eastern part of the state with business interests—was delivered to the state legislature, urging passage of laws to aid southern slave holders in recovering their human property. Escaped slave and abolitionist William Wells Brown noted in 1854, "Colorphobia is more rampart [in Philadelphia] than in the proslavery... city of New York."

His colleague, black abolitionist Samuel Ringgold Ward, noted that even though Philadelphia was an early stronghold of Quaker resistance to slavery, the Quakers generally exhibited bigotry, not allowing blacks in their churches or schools. "Whatever they do for us," he said, "savors of pity, and is done at arms length."[18] Also contributing to an increase in Northern bigotry was an influx of foreign immigrants.

Although rare, the intensity of racial discrimination in the North could even cause escaped slaves to desire a return to their southern plantation

Fugitive Slave Laws and Northern Prejudice

homes, as in the two cases of Virginia slaves reported in *The Liberator* in November of 1849. But by far, the more frequent occurrence was for the still oppressed runaways to seek liberty and equal opportunity outside of the United States.

In Canada, on the wall of the Dominion Bank in Windsor, Ontario, just across the river from Detroit, is a bronze plaque that reads "Here the Slaves Found Freedom." It is perhaps the greatest irony in the four-hundred-year history of the land that became the free and independent republic of the United States, that some of its residents were forced to flee into the monarchy against whom their ancestors had fought for that freedom and independence, in order to find it for themselves.

In going to Canada, former slaves had only a fuzzy idea of what they were going *to*, but a clear idea of what they were running *from*. One month after the September 1850 enactment of the Federal Fugitive Slave Law, the *Toronto Globe* newspaper ran an article that noted that "Families [in the United States] are separating, leaving their homes and flying in all directions to seek protection denied them in the Free Republic."[19]

The estimates agree that approximately sixty thousand black people had fled the United States for freedom in Canada by the start of the Civil War in 1861. By July of 1793, Ontario had enacted a gradual emancipation law to take full effect by 1818. It prohibited slave owners from bringing slaves into the province and assured freedom to any escaped slave who entered.

Britain followed in 1833 by emancipating all slaves throughout the British Empire and refused to extradite former slaves to their country of origin. In Canada, Britain was trying to settle the vast territory there and welcomed immigrants with rights to citizenship, ownership of land, free labor, and the vote. Some communities in the United States lost black residents in droves as they fled the threat of capture.

In Boston, the African Methodist Church lost eighty-five members, the First Baptist Church lost forty of one hundred twenty-five members, and the Twelfth Baptist Church lost sixty of one hundred forty-one.

When We Get to Heaven

5000 Men & Women WANTED,

To attend the Meetings in

Canastota, *Wednesday, Oct. 23d,* 10 a. m.

Cazenovia, *Friday, Oct. 25th,* "

Hamilton, *Wednesday, Oct. 30th,* "

Peterboro, *Friday, Nov. 1st,* "

None but *real* Men and Women are wanted. The sham Men and Women, who can stick to the Whig and Democratic parties, are not wanted. These parties made the accursed law, under which oppressors and kidnappers are now chasing down the poor among us, to make slaves of them. Hence, there is no hope of good from persons, who can stick to these Devil-prompted parties.

We want such men and women to attend these Meetings, as would rather suffer imprisonment and death than tolerate the execution of this man-stealing law. We want such, as would be glad to see William L. Chaplin, now lying in a Maryland prison on account of his merciful feelings to the enslaved, made Governor of the State of New-York. We want, in a word, such noble men and women, as used to gather under the banners of the good old Liberty Party.

Let us, then, get together again to speak the truth, and to sing the truth. Those were good times, when we came together to hear warmhearted speeches for the slave, and to hear Otis Simmons' daughters, and Rhoda Clinek, and Miss Cook, &c. &c., sing

"Come join the Abolitionists."
"What mean ye, that ye bruise and bind?"
"The Yankee Girl."
"There's a good time coming, boys."

October 10, 1850.

This poster called Central New Yorkers to rallies following the adoption of the Fugitive Slave Act in 1850.

Fugitive Slave Laws and Northern Prejudice

The Baptist Colored Church of Buffalo lost one hundred thirty, the Colored Baptist Church of Rochester lost one hundred twelve of one hundred fourteen members, and meetings or conventions of defiance and protest of the 1850 Fugitive Slave Law were held in many northern communities in the United States.[20]

There were many communities in Canada that benefited from immigration of blacks. At the western end of Lake Erie, Windsor, Buxton, and Colchester received immigrants from Detroit and all the way east to Cleveland, Ohio. At the eastern end of Lake Erie were St. Catherine's, Chatham, Dawn, and Wilberforce, and many others scattered along the Canadian border from Michigan to the Montreal area.

Elgin and Dawn were planned communities established by abolitionists and philanthropists specifically for blacks fleeing discrimination and threats within the United States. They emphasized the development of education and religion aimed at making blacks self-reliant models of achievement in an effort to explode myths about black inferiority that were used as arguments in support of slavery. By 1850, St. Catherines, a favorite terminus for Harriet Tubman, had a population that was twelve percent black, and Elgin boasted three hundred black families living prosperously on nine thousand acres of land.

Syracuse, NY Underground Railroad station master Jermain Loguen made several trips to black communities in Canada to check on the progress and stability of former slaves who had passed through his Syracuse station. "I found those who have left this country on account of slavery and its wicked laws doing much better than I had expected," he noted. Loguen noted that immigrants needed support during their first year of adjustment, so he helped to establish a center for such aid just inside the Canadian border to help arriving blacks find shelter and work. He found that some blacks in the urban areas "more than compete with the whites in the acquirement of wealth, intelligence, and the arts of life."[21]

Life in Canada for escaped slaves, however, was not all rosy. Discrimination against blacks continued to the extent that they had to establish their own segregated schools in some communities. They found that the competition for jobs with poor whites aggravated racism. Being unprepared for long and cold winters, many became sick, and the death rate—especially for children—was high. What they did have was political freedom and the guarantee—secured by abolitionists back in the United States—that they could not be extradited, as Gerrit Smith put it, "for a crime committed while in the process of escaping from slavery." Canada refused to extradite a former slave unless he had committed a crime under existing Canadian statutes. And because slavery did not exist in Canada, escaping it could not be viewed as a crime.[22]

The achievement of political freedom in the "Heaven" of northern states or Canada was a bittersweet end to a life's journey for most blacks who attempted it. The power of freedom was enough of a motivation and a reward for them to be willing to undergo hardships in attaining it, but because of continuing racism, the sweetness of freedom was never complete. The determination of slaves to escape bondage was certainly a testimony to their essential humanity. The fact that escape was available at all was in large part the responsibility of a "Band of Angels" called abolitionists who pieced together a network of support for those who dared to escape the bonds of tyranny. This Underground Railroad extended from inside the slave states to Canada, passing through hundreds of villages and hamlets throughout the free states of the North. It was operated by liberal-minded people of all classes and races—including some former runaway slaves.

Examining the experiences of station masters, conductors, passengers, and local residents in a wide range of communities would be a prodigious task, but perhaps it is instructive to look at one such community: the hamlet of Peterboro, NY, home of abolitionist and Underground Railroad station master Gerrit Smith.

Part III

Runaways in Peterboro

Ten

Attitudes and Connections

> "For many years I have regarded the helping of slaves to liberty, especially at the great peril of the helper, as among the most beautiful expressions and among the most decisive evidences of disinterested benevolence and genuine piety."[1]
>
> -Gerrit Smith, 1850

Gerrit Smith lived in the hamlet of Peterboro, town of Smithfield, from the time he was nine years old in 1806 until his death in 1874. As a boy, he saw his father's slave at work around their developing estate. He may have known of the case of Hiram Kellogg, a slave who escaped from his Smithfield owner, Charles Webster, in 1809. Webster advertised for Kellogg's capture in the local newspaper, *The Freeholder,* on April 29, offering a reward and warning against aiding his escape.

Located amid the gently rolling hills of Central New York, Peterboro was a rural hamlet of unique beauty. The two-acre village green bordered by large trees was a frequent focus of activity for residents whose houses and businesses surrounded it.

Gerrit Smith loved "his village" and its physical beauty. "This is another heavenly morning!" he wrote to his wife, Ann, in 1873. "Can it be that there are such mornings anywhere else than in Peterboro?"[2]

A map of routes on the Underground Railroad. The point where the roads crossed in the center of New York State was Peterboro.

In addition to its physical beauty, Peterboro in the 1800s was a place of social vigor. Smith's philanthropic attitude, liberal ideas, and wealth attracted social activists into a melting pot of social change movements that included women's rights, "free" or nonsectarian churches, temperance, politics, and, of course, the abolition of slavery. With more than thirty local businesses and a population of about three hundred and fifty residents, Peterboro was a bustling center from which sprang some of the most enlightened human rights ideas of the nineteenth century.

As Smith matured and grew wealthy from the profits of a land sale business originally developed by his father, he opened his home to escaping slaves as a station on the emerging Underground Railroad. The geographical location of Peterboro in Madison County was important for two reasons. First, it was at the crossroad of two Underground Railroad routes

Attitudes and Connections

that led travellers around the Catskill Mountains. One route went west from Albany, the other north from Binghamton, converging at Peterboro. Second, this location gave Smith the advantage of operating his station at the end of the line; the next stop was usually Oswego, the gateway to Canada and freedom. Smith liked to see immediate, tangible results of his philanthropy, which he preferred to disburse in small amounts at the local level. In Peterboro he saw the success of his efforts, occasionally receiving letters of thanks—and even visits—from former slaves he had aided.

Runaway slaves referred to the northern part of the United States as "Heaven." This label has particular relevance to Peterboro because of an unusual incident from the late 1840s. An educator and radical abolitionist from Troy, NY named Henry Highland Garnet was living temporarily in Peterboro when two former slave women arrived there. Frederick Douglass wrote to Gerrit Smith of his concern for the women's safety due to the activity of slave-catchers. After Smith made him aware of Douglass' concern, Garnet responded, "There are yet two places where slave holders cannot come—Heaven and Peterboro."

Reformer and abolitionist Gerrit Smith dedicated his life to liberal causes. His home in Peterboro became a beacon for slaves on the road to freedom.
From the modern portrait by Joe Flores, commissioned for the National Abolition Hall of Fame & Museum

When We Get to Heaven

The Smith home in Peterboro was a major station on the Underground Railroad in Central New York. Built in 1804, it was destroyed by fire in 1936.

It seems that both slaves and abolitionists knew that in "Heaven," equal human rights were a reality.

Gerrit Smith's belief in the basis of human rights in Natural Law combined with his optimism and his wealth to have an infectious effect on those around him, and Peterboro became a comfortable haven for oppressed people seeking freedom. Within his family, his wife Ann and his two children, Elizabeth and Greene, all heartily supported the Underground Railroad activity. Their letters indicate deep empathy for escaping former slaves, and admiration and approval of their father's work in that arena.

Smith's business clerks were also supportive, especially Caleb Calkins and Federal Dana in Peterboro and John B. Edwards of Oswego. Even Peterboro community residents were aware of and supported the station, sometimes guarding the house during times of threat from encroaching slave catchers. According to one observer of the Peterboro scene,

> "The station at Peterboro was usually full. In times of unusual excitement, like those immediately succeeding the 'Fugitive Slave Bill' [of 1850] it was no uncommon

Attitudes and Connections

thing to see negroes in the street asking the way to Mr. Smith's house.... He was immensely cheated, of course; but he took the cheating patiently, saying that he would rather be swindled twenty times than miss a single chance of delivering a fellow-man."[3]

The combination of Smith's passion for abused people, his wealth, and his family and community support made Peterboro an attractive Underground Railroad station. Transient former slaves seldom stayed in Peterboro for long, but before they departed for Canada, Smith used the opportunity to lecture them regarding habits of temperance, frugality, and morality, perhaps thus fostering his reform efforts in other areas. Some did stay in the Smithfield area, especially before 1850, as evidenced by the fact that the town, although physically the smallest in Madison County, had more African American residents in 1850 than any other town within the county.[4]

When former slaves did take up residence locally, Smith continued his aid by helping them find employment and purchase homes. He felt so

A Peterboro street scene, probably around 1880. The village welcomed a surprising number of important visitors for a community of under 400 people.

107

The Stable Barn, which still stands on the grounds of the Gerrit Smith Estate National Historic Landmark site, housed wagons and horses used to transport the runaway slaves toward Canada. It may have been used to hide slaves as well.
Photo by Brian L. McDowell

confident that they would achieve freedom through the Peterboro connection that he sometimes published detailed accounts of their escape.[5] Creating widespread public knowledge of escapes would, he believed, contribute to the destabilization of the institution of slavery.

Smith also used the medium of writing in his attempt to destabilize slavery. He openly challenged abolitionists to aid escaping slaves,[6] and believed that abolitionists should communicate directly with the slave instead of the slave owner (who probably would not listen anyway).

In a speech to the New York State Abolition Convention in January of 1842, Smith declared,

> "Let abolitionists fully and solemnly utter the doctrine, that they are bound to enter into and maintain all practicable communications with the slave, ... that the abolitionist has a perfect moral right to go into the South, and use his intelligence to promote the escape of

Attitudes and Connections

ignorant and imbruted slaves from their prison-house.... We ... call on every slave who has the reasonable prospect of being able to run away from slavery, to make the experiment.... We rejoice, with all our hearts, in the rapid multiplication of escapes from the house of bondage.... The abolitionist knows no more grateful employment than that of carrying the dog and rifle-hunted slave to Canada."

In this radical effort to communicate with slaves, he continued, "Have no confidence in pro-slavery preachers. Those sham ministers of the Gospel, whether at the North or South, who dare not rebuke oppression, [and] would barter away your souls for one smile of the proud tyrants on whom they fawn.... And when... you are escaping... take all along your route, in the free as well as the slave State, so far as is absolutely essential to your escape, the horse, the boat, the food, the clothing, which you require, and feel no more compunction for the justifiable appropriation than does the drowning man for possessing himself of the plank that floats his way."

Smith authored a resolution passed by the Liberty Party Convention held in Cazenovia on July 3, 1849, which stated that slaves throughout the South should be supplied not with Bibles but with compasses and pistols, and he also advocated his escapee theft of property idea at other antislavery gatherings.[7] In general, he felt that because slaves were oppressed by state and national laws, they were not under obligation to obey them. As president of the New York State Vigilance Committee in the 1840s, Smith lent his name and his money to organized efforts to aid escapees.[8]

Other acts that reflected Smith's attitude toward destabilizing slavery included his willingness and readiness to purchase slaves in order to set them free and his participation in the violent rescue of slaves being held by legal authorities. In 1851, a former slave named Jerry (also known as William Henry), who was working as a barrel maker and living in Syracuse, New York, was captured by federal marshals under the authority of the recently passed 1850 Fugitive Slave Law. They held him for eventual return into southern slavery. Smith, along with Underground Railroad operator Jermain Loguen of Syracuse and other antislavery activists, made a dramatic show of forcibly rescuing Jerry and aiding his escape to Canada.

Some of the rescuers blackened their faces in a Boston Tea Party-like insult to legal authorities, and some women of Syracuse sent thirty Judas-inspired pieces of silver to James R. Lawrence, the government attorney in the case.[9] Gerrit Smith, desiring publicity for the rescue as a shining example of northern opposition to the oppression of human rights, volunteered as Jerry's legal counsel, saying to him, "I am… your friend…. I shall defend you at any expense, and leave no stone unturned to secure your freedom."[10]

Smith actively opposed any man-made law that contradicted natural law, which he argued supported universal human rights:

"If there be human enactments against our entertaining

The Jerry Rescue monument in Clinton Square, downtown Syracuse, NY, depicts the rescue of William Henry, a runaway slave who was also known as Jerry.
Photos by Brian L. McDowell

Attitudes and Connections

the stricken stranger——against our opening our door to our poor, guiltless, and unaccused colored brother pursued by bloodthirsty kidnappers——we must, nevertheless, say with the apostle: 'We must obey God rather than man' "[11]

Smith's attitude in opposing slavery was reinforced by the development in the South of patrols in many local areas to ensure that black people could not escape to the North. The patrollers were usually young, racist men who brutalized blacks who were off the plantation property. Smith saw such patrols as a creation of "terror-stricken whites" who were constantly afraid that their supposedly happy "darkies" would either rebel against them or run away.[12]

If they did run away, the chances were good that they could become involved in an informal web of connections which would aid them on their route toward freedom.

Gerrit Smith's connections on this Underground Railroad network were like those of station masters in many rural locations across the north-

This 1850s illustration depicts a patroller at the moment he discovers a runaway slave with the aid of another black. Such scenes became common on the roads and pathways that made up the Underground Railroad, which slaves traveled at night to conceal their escape.

ern United States—informal and unorganized. As his daughter Elizabeth Smith Miller wrote in a letter to researcher Wilbur H. Siebert, Gerrit was not part of an "organization for sending fugitives to Canada, but aided many who came to him to reach that veritable 'Land of the Free'."[13]

Smith supported the concept of a route to freedom not only through the use of his home, but also by substantial financial expenditures. In 1848, the New York State Vigilance Committee (designed to aid escaping slaves) received a donation of five hundred dollars from Smith. An observer of his Underground Railroad station activity over a period of years estimated that Smith's annual expenditures in aiding the escape of slaves totalled as much as five thousand dollars (five hundred thousand today).[14]

He even argued in person before the New York State Assembly in favor of recognizing the freedom of anyone within New York State borders. "New York," said Smith, "in her sovereign capacity [should] assert her independence as a sovereign State, and by positive enactment, pass such laws as shall protect all persons coming within her jurisdiction."[15]

One of the most important connections Gerrit Smith made was with Harriet Tubman. They were alike in their tactics of operation as they disbursed their philanthropy: both used practical, individually targeted efforts that could lead to quick, visible success. On her several trips north with escaping slaves, Harriet usually followed the same route

> "to Wilmington, where her close friend Thomas Garrett was always waiting with food and friends. From this friendly home she led the way through southern Chester County, Pennsylvania, into Philadelphia before continuing her dangerous journey into upstate New York...."

She then went through the Albany area and west to a station that could connect her with Canada—usually either Smith at Peterboro or Frederick Douglass at Rochester.[16]

Attitudes and Connections

During one of her trips, Smith wrote, Harriet Tubman "sits by my side... [having] returned... from another of her southern expeditions bringing with her 7 slaves."[17] Tubman felt comfortable in Peterboro: "I remember once after I had brought some colored people from the South, I went up to Peterboro to the Big House. Garret [Gerrit] Smith's son Grune [Greene], was going hunting with his tutor and some other boys. I had no shoes. It was Saturday afternoon and—would you believe it?—those boys went right off to the village and got me a pair of shoes...."[18]

In early 1862, when Tubman felt that her safety was in jeopardy due to increasing levels of hostility between North and South, Smith went with her as a protective escort to Canada and followed up by sending her money periodically for her support while she was there.[19]

When the war was over and there was no longer a need for Underground Railroad connections, Harriet and Gerrit still stayed in touch. In 1864 Smith wrote for her a testimonial to her service to blacks and to her country during the war, and in 1868 he underwrote the printing costs of Sarah Bradford's biography of Tubman, which became a source of income for Tubman after its 1869 publication.[20]

Smith's Underground Railroad station was well known in regions south of Peterboro in both New York and Pennsylvania, and other station masters readily sent clients to him. William Still, a successful station master in Philadelphia, met with Smith in 1851; Peter Hitchcock, a Cortland, NY station master, had a valued connection with Smith as well.[21]

To the west in Syracuse, Smith had connections with station master Jermain Wesley Loguen, Unitarian minister Samuel J. May, and attorney Charles B. Sedgwick, all of whom helped to get escapees safely across the lake to Canada. As Smith's grandson Gerrit Smith Miller told Wilbur H. Siebert, "There were friendly abolitionists all the way from [Peterboro] to Oswego and the fugitives were sent by stages."[22]

The Oswego connection was Smith's business agent there, abolitionist John B. Edwards. He also aided clients sent from Loguen in the Syracuse area. Edwards regularly attended antislavery conventions throughout upstate New York, and was well known for his willingness and ability—with Smith's financial help—to help former slaves make it to Canada.[23] With the network of connections in place, freedom-seeking former slaves arrived in Peterboro frequently, and it is possible to document some of those transient travelers.

Eleven

Former Slaves in Peterboro

*Researched in collaboration with
Town of Smithfield Historian Donna Dorrance Burdick*

"It was wonderful what pains he would be at, what trouble he would take, what risks he would incur, what money he would spend, to compass this object [of helping freedom seeking former slaves]," said O.B. Frothingham, an observer of Gerrit Smith's Underground Railroad efforts.

There is much speculation about what may have occurred at many Underground Railroad stations, but few first-person accounts survive to tell us what happened in these most secret locations. In the case of Gerrit Smith's station at Peterboro, there are some credible eyewitnesses to many events.

Frothingham observed Smith's behavior toward runaway slaves, and he continued with his description:

> "The busy man left his affairs and bestowed
> immediate care on his guests; fed them, clothed
> them, gave them money for necessary expenses,
> sent them in his own wagon to Oswego, and saw
> them in safety on their way northward."

Smith's first cousin, Elizabeth Cady—later Elizabeth Cady Stanton—spent some extended time during summers of the 1830s at the Smith estate in Peterboro. She enjoyed the liberal social atmosphere and discussions about discrimination, and attributed her lifelong interest in human rights issues as having its earliest stimulation in Peterboro. She met and spoke with some runaway slaves and said,

> "The slaves... had heard of Gerrit Smith... as one of the safe points *en route* for Canada.... Hence they... felt that they had a right to a place under his protecting roof. On such occasions the barn and the kitchen floor were utilized as chambers for the black man from the southern plantation...."[1]

One of the more well-known cases of a runaway slave who followed the road north to Peterboro involved a man named Dorsey, who escaped from slave owner John Thomson Mason in late 1842. Said Smith, "I learn from Hon. John Thom[son] Mason... that his slave Dorsey has left him. If Dorsey will come to my house, he will hear the good news of his freedom." Dorsey came and Smith aided his further trip to Canada. Between November 1842 and June 1843, Smith and Mason began a series of letters regarding the possibility of Dorsey's return to his owner in exchange for the promise of freedom. Dorsey declined.

John B. Edwards wrote to Smith from Oswego, the final terminal on the road, "The fugitive Dorsey came to me today with your letter. I have put him aboard of a vessel bound for Canada +gave him $1.00."[2]

Many who did escape through Peterboro were only recorded as numbers. Harriet Tubman went through Central New York, probably stopping at Peterboro in 1853 "with nine refugees in tow," and John B. Edwards once affirmed to Smith that "9 fugitives from Slavery's prison left this port last evening for Canada. They were... in much fear that persons were after them. They said they left in a company of 100, + that about 60 of their number were captured before they got out of slave states."[3]

An unidentified writer told the *Albany Patriot* of "four fugitives" who had arrived at his station "last week" and were eager to get "started

Former Slaves in Peterboro

John B. Edwards, of Oswego, NY, was station master on the last stop of the Underground Railroad before slaves crossed Lake Ontario to freedom in Canada. He worked with Gerrit Smith to effect many escapes.
Courtesy of the Oswego County Historical Society

for Gerrit Smith's." There were two couples, one in their thirties and the other in their twenties. Of the older couple, the man was "scarred from his waistbands to his neck—thickly scarred all around his ribs—a deep scar in his breast, where he was stabbed by his master—a large swelling on his head, where he had been struck by the overseer." His wife had given birth to four children, all of whom had died from abuse in the field. The other couple had also been whipped, and had lost one child to abuse.[4]

Another group of fifty slaves came to Smith's attention through letters from L.E. Simmonds, executor of a New Orleans-based will that specified that they were to be freed upon the death of their owner. Simmonds asked if Smith would help them adjust to freedom. When Smith agreed, Simmonds left New Orleans with forty of them. Only ten made it to Peterboro, the others lost along the way to fatigue or disillusionment.[5]

John B. Edwards in Oswego also mentioned this large group, saying, "I was not before aware that you was expecting 40 to 50 Colored people from New Orleans. It will be doubtful about their all finding ready employ here—but when they arrive here I will do the best I can to get them employment."[6]

In another case a few years later, Edwards informed Smith,

> "The young colored man that was at your house last week arrived at my house last evening, I shall keep him a few days to recuperate."[7]

And again,

> "On Saturday last that Slavery Maimed + Branded man + Brother Robert Thompson called on me with his Subscription Books + letters. By considerable effort I raised in this place $31.25 for him + this morning put him on the Steam Boat for Lewiston. He said his family will be here next week and that you told him that you would give him some small house that you own in this place + that you would direct me what one to let him have that his Family can go in when they arrive."[8]

'Scars on Half of His Back'

A shocking runaway slave case in Peterboro that deeply moved Smith emotionally involved two young black men. John Williams and John W. Scott had travelled at night for "between two and three months" before reaching Binghamton, NY. Williams reported before he escaped, " I cannot sleep. I keep thinking of my wife and children." They had been sold away from him, after which he also was sold to a new owner who lived farther south. The night before he and Scott were to be transported south, they both escaped.

From Binghamton, they travelled north to the Cortlandville, New York station of Peter Hitchcock, who transported them in his wagon to Peterboro. Smith said of them, "Their ignorance... especially of geography, exceeds all my former conceptions of the degree of ignorance to which it is possible to reduce a slave." Williams was forty-nine years old and had never been farther from his place of birth than the neighboring plantation. Smith continued,

> "The fugitives exhibited their bare backs to myself and a number of my neighbors. Williams' back is compara-

tively scarred. But, I speak within bounds, when I say, that one-third to one-half of the whole surface of the back and shoulders of poor Scott, *consists of scars and wales resulting from innumerable gashes.* His natural complexion being yellow and the callous places being nearly black, his back and shoulders remind you of a spotted animal."

Smith's emotions and his commitment to antislavery activity reached a high point as he wrote of these two men, "Fugitive slaves have before taken my house in their way, but never any, whose lips and persons made so forcible an appeal to my sensibilities, and kindled in me so much abhorrence of the hell-concocted system of American slavery."[9] Clearly, his passion against the institution of slavery and his compassion for the freedom-seeking former slave ran high.

One tool Gerrit Smith used to aid escaped slaves was education. In 1834, he established in Peterboro a school designed to educate young black men in preparation for their hoped-for future work in the Christian ministry, perhaps in new black colonies in Africa.

The school operated for only three years due to changes in Smith's views regarding abolition. Until 1835, Smith had supported the colonization of slaves in Africa as a technique of dealing with slavery, and the Peterboro school was designed to educate young men who might wish to return there. But in October 1835, when the organizational meeting of the New York State Anti-Slavery Society was dispersed by a proslavery mob in Utica, Gerrit was converted to a new, more aggressive position: he became a champion of 'immediate abolition' and the retention of former slaves in the American homeland. This rendered obsolete the missionary purpose of the school Smith had founded, but some of its students still received a valuable start to impressive professional careers.

Samuel Harrison was born into slavery in 1818 in Georgia and was freed along with his family when he was three years old. His father died when Samuel was young. His mother, concerned about her son's future, had him learn the trade of shoe making, and then enrolled him in Smith's Peterboro Manual Labor School. Such schools were popular at the time because of the belief that both physical and mental health developed together. Students worked at farm labor for part of the day and studied for another part. Samuel liked the Peterboro school, and he was disappointed when it closed. He finished his education at Western Reserve Academy in Ohio, then pursued an illustrious career as a minister, serving as a chaplain during the Civil War and as a pastor for several churches in the Northeast.[10]

Another student, Thomas Potter, was purchased from slavery, liberated by N. Goodsell of Clinton, NY, and sent to Smith's school. In 1842, Potter indirectly testified to the quality of education received there by writing a letter on the subject of racial discrimination:

> "I am one of those who are generally despised by reason of my bearing a black skin not pleasing to the eyes of inhumanity.... [W]e... are the most wretched, degraded and abject set of beings that ever lived... and the white Americans [have] reduced us to a wretched state of slavery.... I therefore ask the whole American people, had I not rather die, or be put to death, than to be a slave to any tyrant who takes not only my own, but my wife and children's lives, by inches?"[11]

Surveillance of the Smith Estate

One of the most interesting stories of a runaway slave at Peterboro is that of Harriet Powell. While on a visit to Syracuse with her owner in October of 1839, Harriet's escape was aided by sympathetic local people. Her owner posted a two hundred dollar reward for her capture, and sent agents to watch the homes of known local abolitionists.

They set up surveillance of Smith's Peterboro home because it was suspected that Harriet would be taken there for protection. Instead, she was shuffled between relatively obscure but safe houses for a few days.

Former Slaves in Peterboro

This 1839 poster hung in Syracuse, NY after the escape of Harriet Powell. It demonstrates the high value ($20,000 in today's currency) placed on the return of slaves.

Dr. John Clarke of Lebanon, NY and his nephew William Clarke wrote to Smith,

> "I... commit to... your care... the *precious, precious* charge that has been for a few short days sheltered beneath my humble roof, from the foul soul catcher of our *detestable* South."

Jermain Loguen of Syracuse noted in his narrative that Harriet Powell was "taken to Mr. Smith and tenderly and carefully secreted and comforted by him and his not less devoted and generous wife."

Smith wrote, "She tarried a day at my house on her way to Canada and appeared to my family and to my neighbors, who visited here...."[12]

While Harriet was at Smith's house, his cousin Elizabeth Cady was also visiting. The two women talked for two hours, an event that had a profound influence on Cady's perception of the importance of the issue of human rights. Elizabeth Smith later wrote of the incident,

> "In Oct. 1839 the 'white slave Harriet' was concealed in the home for some twenty-four hours. In the evening, my father walked with her to the outskirts of the village where his trusty agent Federal Dana was waiting with a conveyance to take her beyond the reach of her master, who we later found, was in close pursuit."
>
> Cady reported that,
> "Dressed as a Quakeress, Harriet started at twilight with one of Mr. Smith's faithful clerks in a carriage for Oswego, there to cross the lake for Canada. The next day her master and marshals from Syracuse were on her track in Peterboro."

As was typical of Smith, he told the slave owner and marshalls that Harriet had spent a day with them in Peterboro and was safely on her way to Canada, then had them stay for dinner to discuss the issue of slavery.[13]

Federal Dana actually took Harriet to Cape Vincent where, after a twenty-hour delay due to bad weather, she boarded a ferry boat bound for Kingston, Upper Canada. Dana wrote that Harriet expressed feelings of gratitude toward the abolitionists who had helped her, "and the trickling tear told that her heart felt far more than her tongue could utter."

Harriet subsequently wrote to abolitionist Rev. Marcus Smith of Watertown, NY, "not all the money in the United States could induce me to return to slavery." She lived for a while with Charlotte Hales, who told Gerrit Smith that Harriet was fine and that she wanted to hear from her mother and sister who were still in the United States. On April 29, 1840, Harriet married Henry Kelly, "a respectable colored man, in good pecuniary circumstances," and between 1841 and 1856, they had eight children.

Through the medium of the *Friend of Man*, Smith informed Mr. Davenport, Harriet's former owner, that she "was abundantly supplied with money and winter clothing by friends, who mingled their tears with hers, and that she wanted to hear from her family."[14]

The fact that Harriet Powell's owner was close behind her as she escaped was not an unusual occurrence to Smith. He seldom let runaways stay in Peterboro for more than a day or two because it was known to owners and their hired slave catchers that Smith's home was a place where they were likely to seek aid. Once, when a South Carolina sheriff accompanied by a slave owner arrived in Peterboro and demanded that Smith surrender fugitive slaves, he told them that, indeed, the former slaves had been there, but were gone toward Canada. The sheriff searched Smith's property, then left.[15]

Because the operation of Smith's Underground Railroad station was well known, he seldom needed to hide runaways. They usually had a meal, received clothes and money, and were transported north. Smith's grandson, Gerrit Smith Miller, was born in 1845. He remembered that as a small boy, when runaways did need to be hidden, he "helped take them to hiding places—sometimes in the garret of the house or... in the hay mows at the barn. After being fed and rested, as the opportunity offered they could be passed on to Oswego where the Captains of lake vessels known to Smith would give them passage to Canada and safety."

Mary Williams, a Peterboro resident when Miller was an old man, wrote, "Mr. Miller told me that when he woke in the mornings he found... escaped slaves in the basement."[16]

One way Smith attracted runaways to his home was by the use of agents he supported as they traveled through the South, encouraging slaves to escape. Alexander Milton Ross, a Canadian abolitionist, posed as an ornithologist in New Orleans, and while visiting slave owners, would give advice to slaves on how to escape and where to go. When he succeeded in his persuasive efforts, he would alert Smith to be on the lookout for " 'packages of hardware' (men) or 'dry goods' (females) ...."

The escape of John Tyler was arranged by Smith's paid agent in Maryland. "Posing as cattle drovers, abolitionist agents employed by New

York's Gerrit Smith had visited his plantation in eastern Maryland. They instructed Tyler and ten members of his family to leave their cabins after dark and meet them in the woods.... The abolitionists... were able to bring them safely through Pennsylvania to New York." Tyler reported that the group traveled at night and hid in the forest during daylight.

"On Sunday afternoon we could see the master and fifty men with clubs and dogs out looking for us." Station master Thomas Garrett helped them on their route north. Tyler lived in Peterboro and worked for Smith for a while, calling him "a great man." Tyler stayed in central New York, dying in Canastota at the age of one hundred three in 1915.[17]

Another runaway slave who arrived in Peterboro via the Underground Railroad was Hanson Williams. He was born in Maryland and served as a slave of William Figzhugh, Gerrit's brother-in-law. He arrived in Peterboro in 1861, then served in the Civil War as a member of a white cavalry regiment. After the war, he returned to Peterboro and worked for Gerrit Smith, and after Smith's death, as Gerrit Smith Miller's farm foreman for over two decades. Williams died in 1911.[18]

Lewis Washington was also born into slavery in Maryland, escaped from slavery in Virginia, and eventually became a resident of Peterboro. In 1844, he was an antislavery lecturer in the Albany area working with James Caleb Jackson, an abolitionist friend of Gerrit Smith. By 1846, Madison County deed records show that he was a Peterboro property owner, having purchased it from Smith. Washington and Jackson became active on the Liberty Party speaking circuit in Central New York, and Frothingham mentions having seen "A runaway slave, Lewis Washington by name, also his wife [Catharine, and] one or more relatives" dining with Smith at his home. The Washingtons had a child in Peterboro, Julia Lewis Washington, born on April 5, 1847.[19]

Billy and Alden Maxwell Smith

Billy Smith was born as a slave on a Virginia plantation near Richmond. In 1861, during the early stages of the Civil War, he was rescued from slavery by Captain Aaron Bliss of the 10th New York Cavalry. Bliss was a Madison County resident whose father, Lyman Bliss, was an abolitionist friend of Gerrit Smith. After the war, Billy Smith became a resident of Peterboro and was well known for his skill at playing music at public gatherings.[20]

Billy Smith's great-grandson, Alden Maxwell Smith, an accomplished singer, currently lives near Peterboro in the city of Oneida. He frequently sings Negro spirituals at historic events in the area.

When Margaret Ward escaped from slavery on a Maryland plantation in 1830, she took her infant son Samuel with her. In search of a good education for Samuel, she sent him to Peterboro, where he lived with the Smiths while he obtained his education. Samuel Ringgold Ward later became a noted black abolitionist.[21]

While visiting his wife Ann's family—the Fitzhughs—in Rochester in 1837, Gerrit met a slave named John Roberts. John was in the company of his owner, Richard Stockton. Gerrit encouraged John to escape to Canada and assisted him in doing so.[22]

Such stories of former slaves who were helped by Gerrit Smith are many, and are fairly typical of similar cases connected with hundreds of Underground Railroad stations. Some of the desperate runaways are unnamed. Smith referred to some of them in his diary:

"An Indian and a fugitive slave spent last night with us."

"A man . . . brings his mother, six children and her half sister, all fugitives from Virginia."

"There came this evening an old black man, a young one and his wife and infant. They say that they are fugitives form North Carolina."[23]

Escapees went through Peterboro quickly on their way north, and most probably left no trace by which we can research them. John Roberts did send Smith a letter of thanks for aid in achieving his freedom,[24] and we know that escaped slave Austin Bethel was being protected in Peterboro by Smith while a friend negotiated with his former owner in an attempt to buy freedom papers.[25]

When We Get to Heaven

Billy Smith (above, left) and friend Bill Russel played and sang for years throughout Central New York. The photograph is from 1920. Smith became a Peterboro resident after he won his emancipation. His great-grandson, Alden Maxwell "Max" Smith (picture at right), continues the legacy today. Max sang at the 2006 commemoration ceremony of the National Abolition Hall of Fame and Museum, as Gerrit Smith, Frederick Douglass, Harriet Tubman (pictured on banner), William Lloyd Garrison, and Lucretia Coffin Mott were recognized as the first inductees of the hall.

Photo by Brian L. McDowell

Former Slaves in Peterboro

Letters from John B. Edwards to Smith tell of escaped slave Benjamin Hockley from Tennessee who, in 1850, was in the process of purchasing a house and lot in Oswego from Smith. Instead, he went to Canada due to the threat of capture following passage of the 1850 Fugitive Slave Law. It is a fair speculation that he went through Peterboro on his way to Oswego, carrying advice from Smith regarding residence and employment there. He intended to return to his Oswego property when it appeared safe to do so.[26]

Escaped slave George Weedon had received aid in Peterboro on his way to Canada, and because Smith had requested knowledge of his success there, Weedon had a letter written to Smith for him that was printed in the *Albany Patriot* indicating that he "sends respects to you for the kindness shown him." The letter also contained a note for his former owner Mr. Lovinla Lewis of Bethel Town, Clark County, Virginia:

> "I [am] in the dominions of the Queen Victoria, where I can own myself, and be your property no longer.... I hope you will give my kind love to my wife and mother and sisters [and] brothers and to all inquiring friends. I would not have absconded as I did, if it had not been for fear of being sold, and for your allowing your overseers to knock your slaves down, and nearly kill them, whether they had done anything or not...."[27]

This letter eloquently expressed the priorities in an oppressed person's mind: Freedom was more important to Weedon than his family and all the love that must have existed there.

A hint by escaped slave Walter Freeman, whom Smith knew and who probably received aid in Peterboro, appears in a letter to Smith from John F. Cook of Washington, D.C. in which he enclosed a letter from Freeman's wife to be forwarded to him. The presumption was that Smith knew where Freeman was.[28]

An incident that illuminates Smith's treatment of runaway slaves in Peterboro was reported in Frederick Douglass' paper in September of

1853 by a visitor to the Smith estate who signed as "S.P.Q.R." The visitor was from Auburn, New York, and reported the incident as follows:

> "A few hours after I reached Peterboro, Mr. Smith was informed . . . that a person wished to see him. He was absent a few minutes; and returned to the library, bringing with him a poor wayfaring black man, who, doubtless, was fleeing from a land of slavery to one of freedom. He looked at first, timid and ill at ease. Mr. Smith seated him, and began to converse with him. He soon satisfied himself that the man's story was true, and it was beautiful to witness the kind and sympathizing interest evinced by Mr. Smith in the man and his fortunes. He did not content himself by coldly saying, 'be warmed and fed,' etc., but I saw him go to his own wardrobe and find clothing for the fugitive, then he ordered him a bath and commended him to the kind care of good and faithful domestics who did his bidding with alacrity, and made all comfortable for their fortunate guest. I assure you that when the [black] man reappeared in the library, in the evening he seemed a new creature; all traces of the slave had vanished and a free man stood before us, his honest, black face beaming with happiness, present and prospective . . . . I watched the happy smiles which irradiated Mr. Smith's always benevolent countenance, and I felt that he truly enjoyed 'the luxury of doing good'."[29]

In the Spring of 1842, Smith received in Peterboro four runaway slaves from the Maryland plantation of owner John Thomson Mason. When Mason wrote to Smith inquiring about their northward journey, Smith replied with a lengthy letter that beautifully described the attitude of even well-treated slaves, and the process of their accomplishment of freedom. Smith told Mason,

Former Slaves in Peterboro

"The slaves called themselves Jack Johnson (the father) Daniel, Abraham +Franklin (the sons). They spent a day at my house. I was pleased with their good sense + civility.... I am happy to be able to say to you, that the slaves all concurred in the remark made by one of them, that they had been very kindly used by your family, and that nothing but the fear of their being sold prompted them to run away.

"The slaves represented, that, on a Saturday morning, they obtained permission to go to Hagerstown to Church, + that instead of going to Hagerstown, they reached Chambersburgh the next morning. From that place they came to Harrisburgh, Wilkesbarre, + Binghamton. They further represented that they had $22 when they left home, + $4 when they reached my house. They were well clothed. After they had spent a day with me, I added a few dollars to their scanty funds, + sent them in my wagon to the Erie Canal, with directions on whom to call at Syracuse + Oswego. I was in Oswego a week or two after— + I learnt from Mr. Henry Fitzhugh, a brother of Mrs. Smith, that they spent a few hours at his house, and were well. They left Oswego in a Steam Boat for Toronto, Upper Canada. The poor fellows had great hopes that they should find in Canada the other son who ran away five years ago....

"I obtained strong promises from the slaves that they would totally abstain from intoxicating liquors, would be industrious, frugal and virtuous. May the Lord's blessing rest upon them! There are about 1,500 colored people in the Upper Province—almost all runaways and their children. The abolitionists of the U. States are doing what they can to supply them with schools + religious instruction. I wish you could see their present condition, so that you might compare it with what they have left. But I trust, that you need not <u>see</u> their new born liberty to increase your sense of its value + to increase your abhorrence of slavery."[30]

Sometimes Smith was able to help former slaves with money even if they did not come to his home. John Lagrow and Mahommah Gardo Baquaqua were both students at New York Central College in McGrawville in the early 1850s when they asked Smith for financial help in purchasing items such as clothes or land. Both had come from Africa as slaves aboard ships, and then escaped. Obliviously, they knew of Smith's reputation for aiding those seeking freedom.[31]

Another case in which "Smith remembered the man and the incidents of his escape" was that of a runaway slave named Anderson who, en route to Canada from Kentucky, had killed his former owner who was pursuing him. Smith traveled to Canada in order to defend Anderson against extradition to Kentucky, and won the case. It is not clear that Anderson traveled through Peterboro, but certainly Smith's support flowed to *all* in need—not just those who came by way of his house.[32]

A speculative case involves a note dated "Peterboro, Sept. 2, 1843" that appeared in the *Liberty Press*. The note included escaped slave Lewis Clark's itinerary for future speaking engagements throughout Madison County, encompassing fifty-five days during which Clark "will tell all who wish to hear, the wrongs heaped upon the slave as he himself has seen and felt."[33] The note was probably from Smith, as it matched his style of writing and he was most likely the source of support for Clark's speaking tour.

Station master Jermain Loguen of Syracuse wrote of Gerrit Smith's Underground Railroad work in a letter to William Still regarding runaways sent to Loguen from Philadelphia. He mentioned two by name and noted that "Gerrit Smith [is] with others."[34]

The case of a slave named Robert owned by Mr. Dudley of Maysville, KY shows the opportunistic nature of some of Smith's aid to escapees.

Former Slaves in Peterboro

Dudley and Robert had traveled to Utica, NY and were staying in a hotel when Dudley left Robert in the charge of the hotel bartender during his absence. Smith, who was in Utica at the time, was introduced to Robert and offered him an opportunity to escape from his owner. Robert agreed to the deal and was given fifteen dollars by Smith and sent to Peterboro for support and further directions.[35]

A process that does not directly involve Underground Railroad activity but does serve to indicate Smith's attitude toward slavery and those oppressed by it is the purchase of slaves. Smith was openly criticized by other abolitionists for wasting his money on the extravagant purchase of freedom for a few slaves when that money might be put to better uses in the cause of abolition. But because he had considerable wealth and an intense desire to use it in ways that produced quick, visible results, he was attracted to the purchase alternative.

As early as 1836, Smith paid John Thomson Mason of Hagerstown, MD one thousand dollars to purchase the freedom of some of Mason's slaves, and again in 1846, he did the same thing. One of Mason's slaves with a notoriously bad reputation for resistance was William Lee. Smith perceived Lee as a challenge and offered special treatment for him, as reflected in the following letter.[36]

> Peterboro, Nov 21, 1845
> Mr. William Lee:
>
> *Dear Sir,* —— Your master, Mr. Mason writes me that you are a very bad man, and that the best thing to do with you is to sell you to a severe southern master. I take pity on you as my brother man, and send Mr. Mason one hundred and sixty dollars. Ten dollars of the one hundred and sixty, I ask him to hand you to bear your expenses here. The remaining one hundred and fifty dollars are for himself. He consents to part with you for that sum.

> I write Mr. Mason to direct you to my home. I shall not be here when you arrive. I hope to find you in a good family in my neighborhood when I return.... I do not wish you to return me a single dollar of the one hundred and sixty dollars which you cost me. You must be content with small wages in the winter, and to be industrious, sober and good-tempered, you will soon command good wages and have money enough to buy yourself a little home.
> William! I don't believe that the best thing to do with you was to sell you to a hard master. I believe that the best thing for you was to make you a freeman, and now that you are a freeman, you will prove yourself to be a good man, an industrious man, an honest man, a kind-tempered man. Now William, show your old master what a good man a bad slave is capable of becoming when he has freedom.
> Come to see me, William, when I get home. The Lord bless and guide you, and give you good heart.
>
> Your friend,
GERRIT SMITH.

Throughout the antebellum era, Smith purchased freedom for slaves when the opportunities occurred. He realized that he was sometimes duped by slave owners who sold to him old or sick slaves just to get rid of them, but Smith said that he would rather be duped than miss an opportunity to do the right thing for even one slave. Sometimes his purchase offer was refused by the owner, and sometimes even refused by the slave due to suspicion that Smith could be just another oppressor in disguise. In 1837, Carter Braxton of Virginia refused Smith's offer to purchase all of Braxton's slaves.[37]

The most notable and successful purchase of slaves by Gerrit Smith involved the Russell family. When Gerrit's wife Ann Fitzhugh Smith became concerned about the status of a former slave of the Fitzhugh family,

Former Slaves in Peterboro

Gerrit tried to locate that person with the goal of purchasing her freedom. When the slave was located in Kentucky, Smith learned that she had a husband and five children.

An abolitionist friend of Smith, Quaker James Canning Fuller of Skaneateles, was sent to Kentucky in 1841 as an agent to purchase the family and bring them to Peterboro. Their owner, S. Worthington, described himself as being "to some extent opposed to slavery." But he added that he believed that "black people... are... [in]capable of enjoying liberty." Worthington offered to sell the slave family to Smith for four thousand dollars. Fuller negotiated the deal, paid Worthington three thousand five hundred dollars, and departed with some of them for the return trip to Peterboro. Because blacks were not allowed to ride in public con-

Malvina "Vinny" Russell was the youngest of five Russell children and the last former slave to live in Peterboro, NY. She is shown here seated on the back steps of the Cottage Across the Brook, home to Gerrit Smith Miller, where the author lives today.

veyances with whites, Fuller purchased a stage coach—horses included—and traveled north.

Smith eventually informed Worthington of the Peterboro arrival of Fuller with Harriet Russell and three girls who had told him of Worthington's kindness as a slave owner. Smith speculated,

> "If a slave family treated with such eminent kindness, were so eager to embrace the offer of liberty, how must the great mass of Southern slaves pant for that precious boon!"

The Russells settled in the local area, found employment, and eventually purchased land from Smith. Harriet worked for many years in "The Laundry" as laundress for the Smith family. The building still stands on the newly created Gerrit Smith Estate National Historic Landmark site. Descendants of the Russell family still live in Peterboro.[38]

Smith also purchased the freedom of other slaves when he felt that he could afford to do so. In 1849, he paid seventy-five dollars toward the purchase of the brother and child of George R. Williams, and during his stay in Washington, D.C. as a congressman, he contributed money on twenty-five occasions toward the purchase of the freedom of slaves.[39]

Smith's business records reveal other examples of the purchase of slaves' freedom, even during the severe economic depression of 1837 to 1844:

> 1. Four hundred fifty dollars paid to Mr. Woodbin for one slave. "My Heart yearns toward him. I want to comfort him–and I want to see him usefully employed at the North."[40]
> 2. During 1841, "I have paid the present year between four + five thousand dollars in the purchase of the liberty of slaves."[41]
> 3. September 28, 1842 – a note in Smith's handwriting: "I buy 9 slaves at $750.00 per slave - $6,750.00."[42]
> 4. Five hundred dollars paid to Mr. Davis to purchase one slave called "the captain."[43]

Former Slaves in Peterboro

While no longer structurally safe to enter, The Laundry where Harriet Russell worked for Gerrit Smith still stands. It is located next to the Stable Barn (background, right side of photo) on the Gerrit Smith Estate National Historic Landmark site. *Photo by Brian L.*

His attitude toward this use of his money was clear in a letter to a southern friend and observer of slavery, in which he wrote of "the great delight I take in purchasing the Liberty of slaves.... None of my expenditures of money have brought me more gladness of heart."[44]

Ezekiel Birdseye was an abolitionist friend of Smith who lived in Tennessee. At one point he acknowledged the receipt of four hundred fifty dollars from Smith to be used in the purchase of a slave's freedom.[45] Even if fraud was suspected, as in the case of "fugitive slave" Mrs. Lee of Rochester, Smith offered money and letters of support rather than miss a chance to help someone.[46]

When We Get to Heaven

Calling Their Bluffs

A radical example of Smith's interest in purchasing the freedom of slaves surfaced in a speech made by Frederick Douglass in London, England in 1847. Some slave owners in the South who claimed to be opposed to the moral principle of slavery indicated that they had not freed their own slaves because they could not afford to do so. In response to that point, Gerrit Smith, Arthur Tappan (a wealthy abolitionist in New York City) and "other noble- minded abolitionists" published in newspapers the offer of a fund of ten thousand dollars dedicated to purchasing the freedom of slaves owned by persons who wanted to free them but were restrained from doing so by personal economic pressures. It appears that this effort to "call the bluff" of hypocritical slave owners worked: not one slave owner ever applied for the available funds.[47]

For those who continued north from Peterboro in their quest for freedom, Smith supplied their needs generously. Whereas their staples were easy for Smith to provide, safe transportation was not; there were always enterprising proslavery people nearby who would readily turn in a fugitive slave for the posted reward. The *Liberty Herald* reported an 1844 case of an escaped slave who had settled in Orange County, OH and was recognized by a visitor. His neighbors, informed of this, captured him and delivered him to his former owner for the monetary reward.[48]

The last leg of the journey to Canada involved the relatively short trip from Peterboro to Oswego, where runaways could secure water transport to Canada. According to Gerrit Smith Miller, Ann Fitzhugh Smith liked to take a daily ride through the countryside near Peterboro in a closed buggy with a driver.

> "If on certain occasions her place was occupied by a veiled figure who sat far back in the shadow, inquisitive people had no reason to suspect that it was not Lady Smith taking her daily drive."

Caleb Calkins was hired by Gerrit Smith as a young man because of his abolitionist opinions. He spent his entire career as Smith's business clerk in Peterboro.

"One [runaway] was dressed in my grandmother's driving outfit and was driven to Oswego by Caleb Calkins [Smith's business clerk] in my grandfather's buggy...."

Although Smith realized that many of the freed slaves whom he helped would not adjust well to their new life, he did not hesitate to give them the opportunity. In fact, on the whole, runaway slaves who went to Canada were recognized as a

"superior class of colored people [who have] had a favorable influence on the minds of many who had judged all of the whole from the unhappy specimens which [U.S.] cities too abundantly supply."[49]

When We Get to Heaven

Humble Surroundings

The following is adapted from Practical Dreamer: A Biography of Gerrit Smith, *Norman K. Dann's 2009 work.*

It is a humble structure, the very sort that probably housed Underground Railroad stops all along the routes that led from southern states to freedom.

Inside this small brick land office is a single room measuring twenty-five by twenty feet, with a brick floor laid on top of a wood frame. A six-inch round hole in the chimney wall shows where the wood stove stood. Gerrit's desk was on a raised platform across the room from the stove. He spent fifty-five years doing the work of his land business in this room. If a modern-day visitor listens carefully through the soft rain, he might hear voices.

Gerrit Smith's office still stands on the grounds of the Gerrit Smith Estate National Historic Landmark site, right off the village green in Peterboro. A marker notes the history of the place. In the background is the Stable Barn, where Smith stored horses and wagons used to transport runaway slaves to Syracuse, Oswego, and other points on the Underground Railroad.
Photo courtesy of the National Abolition Hall of Fame & Museum

Former Slaves in Peterboro

He might see Harriet Tubman in her tattered shoes sitting by the south window, quietly asking for aid and advice on helping twelve fugitive slaves reach safety in Canada. One of the slaves, a young, very dark male, sits next to her. He looks frightened and happy at the same time.

There, by the warm stove, stands John Brown, his eyes sparkling as he reveals to Gerrit his latest plans for a free Kansas and asks for money to buy supplies for his next trip west.

Frederick Douglass stares dreamily through the east window at the Smith mansion. He speaks over his shoulder to Gerrit of his own glorious feeling of freedom and his satisfaction in aiding the cause of abolition through his newspaper, *The North Star*. His stature, with arms folded and muscles tense, elicits the determination of an obsessed man, a national leader, a black Abraham Lincoln destined to succeed.

In the wooden chair beside Gerrit's desk sits a middle-aged man, hat in hand, who has just walked five miles from Clockville to negotiate a postponement of his payments.

In front of the desk stands a defiant Kentucky slave owner who has traveled north searching for his fugitive property. After his shouts have filled the small room with harshness and threats, Gerrit invites him to stay for dinner.

Over half a million acres of land changed ownership in this room, grossing probably over one billion dollars in today's money. Yet the most important symbol of this land office is its humility.

The Gerrit Smith Estate was selected in 2002 by the National Park Service as a National Network to Freedom Underground Railroad Site. And in 2004 it was named part of the New York State Underground Railroad Heritage Trail.

Looking Back

As we of the twenty-first century watch the increase of terrorist incidents in the world, we sometimes forget about the lifetime of terror facing slaves in this country for two and a half centuries. Gerrit Smith's efforts to help former slaves seek the freedom they craved was sincere, extravagant, and endless—especially through the operation of his Underground Railroad station at his home.

One historian and author on the Underground Railroad has labeled Smith as "the most powerful abolitionist in the country...."[50] Perhaps this is true, for the combination of his attitude toward human rights and his money lubricated the successful operation of the Underground Railroad at his Peterboro station.

There, he risked everything he had for people he did not know in a cause he could not resist. From north to south, hundreds of other Underground Railroad station masters did the same. If the pull of freedom was powerful to the slave who sought a road out of bondage, it was powerful as well to the station master who forfeited fortune and friendships to help the slave start new a life.

The station master's rewards were often uncollected. They received thanks, but little positive recognition; they would not even know the fates of most of the people they aided. Yet in a sense, the success of the Underground Railroad is measured in the silence with which its travelers and conductors went about the business of aiding freedom-seekers..

The tiny hamlet of Peterboro welcomed abolitionists of national prominence and was home to one of the most influential abolitionists of his time. It is an ideal place to house the National Abolition Hall of Fame.

End Notes

One

1. Aptheker 46
2. *Larson, 54*
3. Pettit 42-43
4. Campbell, E. 2, 3
5. Aptheker 17
6. quoted in Sanborn v
7. Douglass 152; Jefferson also understood this. See Miller 41
8. Douglass 191
9. Douglass 269, 272
10. Kolchin 138
11. Kolchin 138-140
12. Foner, *A Short*... 36
13. *Runaway*...262, 165, 169, 249
14. Franklin 274-279
15. Dumond 192
16. Sept. 13, 1835, quoted in Fladeland 122

Two

1. Korbin 20, 22
2. Fox H4; Dumond 4
3. Lester 25
4. Horton, *Slavery* ... 26, 27
5. *The Abolitionist*, Nov. 22, 1842 7, c. 1
6. Clinton 10, 11; Smith, William 3; Stampp, *The Peculiar*... 245
7. *Liberty Herald*, Oct. 30, 1844
8. Stampp, *The Peculiar*... 271, 272; Shaw 203, 204
9. Shaw 158-162

10. Dumond 315; see also Litwack 4-7; Stampp, *The Peculiar*... 204, 212
11. Shaw 157, 167, 168
12. Dumond 57
13. Wiecek 59; Dumond 315; Dillon 18; Stampp, *The Peculiar*... 28
14. Tate 91, 98
15. Tate 91, 98: Gerrit Smith to Rev. James Smylie, Oct. 28, 1836, PHS
16. Dumond 8, 9; Miller 144; Higginson 254; Horton, *Slavery*...30
17. Dumond 11, 66, 95, 179; Stampp, *The Peculiar* ...88; Aptheker 67.
18. Smith 14-16; Clinton 101
19. Parker 91
20. Shaw 163
21. Harrold 19; Dumond 27
22. Korbin 8-10
23. Stewart, 62-64
24. Dumond 11
25. Groth 36, 41, 44-46.
26. Phelan 18; Painter 108; Nordstrom 19, 20
27. Shaw 264, 265

Three

1. Mayer 153
2. Campbell, E. 25; Smith 37
3. quoted in Smith 37, 38
4. Miller 106, 107
5. Yellin 183
6. Loguen 179
7. Dumond 288
8. Douglass 185, 186
9. Foner, *Free Soil*... 43, 52, 53
10. Lowance 165
11. Kolchin 175-177, 181

End Notes

12. Osofsky 65, 67, 74
13. Address to the American Colonization Society, 1829 quoted in Lowance 94-96, 99
14. Lowance 41, 42
15. Lester 18: Franklin, *From Slavery...* 54
16. Dumond 147
17. quoted in Dumond 355
18. Brandt 140
19. Wish 179; Foner, *Free Soil...* 66, 67.
20. see Gerrit Smith papers, Department of Special Collections, Syracuse University Library
21. Kolchin 191-197
22. Perry 25
23. Lowance 109, 110
24. Harrold 117
25. Miller 104
26. Steward 10
27. Miller 50
28. Weld 117, 111
29. Northup 184; Osofsky 338
30. Kashatus 9; Weld 112
31. Weld 170, 171; Stampp, *The Peculiar...* 17; Blockson 88, 89
32. Miller 221-223; Kolchin 198, 199
33. Dumond 75, 357, 358
34. Dillon 66, 67; Foner, *Free Soil* ...99

Four

1. Lester 107
2. Douglass 64, 275
3. Washington 78
4. Douglass 175, 183

5. Shaw 166, 174, 175; Rose 395
6. Kashatus 17
7. Douglass 60
8. Yetman106; Franklin, *From Slavery*...10; Weld 36, 38
9. Northup 164-166.
10. Botkin 75
11. Botkin 55
12. Douglass 104, 105
13. Stevenson
14. viewed in artist John W. Jones' paintings, 2003
15. Kolchin 101, 107, 108
16. 221
17. Yetman 66
18. Yetman, 67, 106; Weld 37; Northup 170
19. Weld 28, 31, 95; Stampp, *The Peculiar* ... 285; Yetman 74; Steward 3; Northup 168, 171
20. Gates 72; Stampp, *The Peculiar*... 290, 292; Weld 40-42, 95
21. 70
22. Stampp, *The Peculiar*... 298-318; Clinton 16; Weld 45; Parker 97
23. Botkin 178
24. Aptheker 7; Stampp, *The Peculiar*... 294, 295; Weld 43; Northup 170
25. Douglass 62-64
26. in Rose 337
27. *The Liberator*, July 20, 1849 114
28. Blockson, *National*...5; Lester 77; Stamp, *Rebels*...
29. Lester 101, 102; Dumond 45; Korbin 33; Aptheker 6
30. Franklin, *From Slavery*...151, 152; Stampp, *The Peculiar*... 142-131; Clinton 44
31. Yellin 101
32. Lester 100; Osofsky 9; Still 122; Franklin, *Runaway*... 149
33. Franklin, *From Slavery*... 2-6; Stampp, *The Peculiar*... 100-104; Lester 99; Kolchin 155-166

Five

1. Weld 7, 8
2. Weld 53, 57, 62, 117, 125
3. Steward 9, 51
4. Botkin 43
5. Weld 60
6. Shaw 176; Weld; Rose 197
7. Mabee 140; Stevenson 28
8. Douglass 85, 102-105
9. Northup 224; Steward 5
10. Botkin 91
11. Douglass 80
12. Rose 213
13. Yetman 5; Loguen 123, 124
14. Franklin *From Slavery*...50; Weld 60; Stevenson 38; Lester 72
15. Loguen 114-119
16. Weld 46, 47; Roper 22, 23; Lowance 228, 319; Franklin *From Slavery* ... 51, 52
17. Stampp, *The Peculiar*...172-188
18. Botkin 187
19. Roper 8
20. Rose 52
21. Stampp, *The Peculiar*...161; Larson 47-53; Weld 26; Kolchin 146-148

Six

1. Northup 249
2. Fladeland 115
3. Rose 106

4. Miller 10,11
5. Aptheker 11-13
6. Franklin, *From Slavery*... 183; Mabee 55
7. July 28, 1861
8. Aptheker 43
9. Aptheker 71
10. Oates; Perry 5, 6; Aptheker 17-20; Dumond 109-113; Rose 99-115; Harrold 16, 23; Parker 31; Tate 110-113.
11. Oates 154
12. Gates 128
13. Douglass 263, 264; Schor.
14. Tate 44, 56, 65-87
15. Franklin, *Runaway* ... 282; Gates 121
16. Botkin 92; Yellin 113
17. Franklin, *Runaway*... 86-165
18. Larson 24, 25, 130, 150, 151
19. Gara, "The Fugitive..." 230; Franklin, *Runway*... 264; Brandt 146
20. Franklin, *Runaway* ... 38, 234, 235, 242, 243
21. Franklin, *Runaway*... 103

Seven

1. *Friend of Man*, July 28, 1836 24
2. see Gara, *The Liberty Line*, 2-17; Gara, "Myth and Reality"
3. Ripley 45; Franklin, *From Slavery*...; Scruggs 113; Blockson 29; Gara, "A Glorious Time"...284
4. no author, *The Reverend*... 28; similar sentiments are also found in Quarles 226; Still 2; Steward 69.
5. 40
6. Dumond 364,365
7. Bordewich, "Free..." 69.
8. Turner 309, 310

End Notes

9. Franklin, *Runaway*... 109-122.
10. Kobrin 34-41; Phelan 17
11. Blockson, *The Underground*...205, 206
12. Klees 100; Parker 79; Still 2, 107, 301, 368; Franklin, *Runaway*... 117, 224-227; Bordewich, *Bound*...117
13. Horton, H.D.
14. Parker 71, 72, 99, 187-189; Franklin, *Runaway*... 210-212; Hunter 38; Kashatus 15; Johnson 422-425
15. Phelan 137

Eight

1. Blockson, *The Underground*...83
2. Clinton 62
3. Phelan 75; Blockson, *The Underground*... 230, 234; Ripley 59; Quarles 153; Clinton 54; Shaw 243
4. *Friend of Man*, Sept.1, 1836 43
5. Quarles 157, 159; *Albany Patriot*, June 25, 1844, 130-131
6. Mabee 60; Wiltse xii
7. Mabee 56; Gara, "The Fugitive ..." 236; Frothingham 190; Mc Feely 211
8. Mabee 374; Mayer 320
9. Phelan 78, 90, 93; Blockson, *The Underground*... 190, 197; Sernett, *North Star*... 176-178; Alilunas; Sturge 53; Bordewich, *Bound*... 230
10. Mabee 280; Blockson, *The Underground*... 208, 214, 215; Gara "Friends and ..." 13
11. Hunter 42, 153, 154, 157; Pettit 34; Loguen 392, 393
12. Still 158, 221, 426, 517
13. Klees 99; Still 193; Blockson, *The Underground*... 233
14. Still 632; Gara, "Friends and..." 9; Larson 103
15. *Friend of Man*, July 24, 1839 24
16. letter, Gerrit Smith to the editor of the *Union Herald*, reprinted in

Friend of Man, Dec 1, 1838; *The Liberator*, Nov 30, 1849 189; also in Franklin, *Runaway*... 191, 193

17. Parker 33-35; Franklin, *Runaway*... 111-113
18. Parker 183-186
19. Yetman 23, 26
20. Mabee 279
21. Horton H. D. 128-137
22. Blockson, *The Underground*...198; Phelan 130; Bordewich, "Free... 69
23. Clinton 85, 85, 94
24. Lester 105
25. Botkin 177
26. Gerrit Smith to James Smylie, Oct. 28, 1836, PHS; Shaw 181; Northup 237
27. Weld 145; Pettit 153; Dummond 316, 318, 406, 407
28. Hunter 159; Kashatus 31; Douglass; Letter Hiram Wilson to *Friend of Man*, July 12, 1839 22.
29. Northup 33, 34, 61, 62
30. Mabee 275; Larson 88; Kashatus 30
31. Dumond 336
32. Loguen; Still 348-357
33. Weld 21, 23, 161
34. Yanuck 47; Blockson, *The Underground*...217-223; Bordewich, *Bound*...119
35. Blockson, *The Underground*...189
36. Ripley; Still 51-53; Clinton 34; Gates 124
37. Levy 68
38. Ripley 46, 47

End Notes

Nine

1. Dumond 310
2. Franklin, *Runaway*...151; Franklin, *From Slavery* ...57; Parker 30-49
3. Franklin, *From Slavery* 160, 161
4. quoted in Thornbrough 201
5. Goodheart 86; Ripley 51
6. Alilunas 166, 167; *Liberty Herald*, Nov. 16, 1843 1
7. Blockson, *The Underground*... 230; Quarles 225; Alilunas 167; Finkleman 6-8, 14, 123, 124, 137; Dumond 307-309
8. Shaw 239
9. Dumond 321; Clinton 54, 55.
10. Dillon 176; Eggert; Gara, *The Fugitive* ...235; Douglass 453; Mabee 291, 301
11. Gara, "The Fugitive..." 235; Franklin, *Runaway*... 174-178, 217, 218; Clinton 67; Ripley 63; Parker 196-201; Rose 22, 23; Campbell, E. 199-202, 207
12. Shaw 248
13. Clinton 39
14. letter, Loguen to Frederick Douglass, quoted in Loguen 339, 340
15. Sterling 143
16. Dumond 11; Stampp, *The Peculiar*... 153; Wilson 339
17. Clinton 47-53
18. Blockson "Escape From...30; Turner 318; Blockson, *The Underground* ...229
19. Dumond 335; Clinton 101; *Toronto Globe* Oct. 15, 1850
20. Blockson, *The Underground*...287; Dumond 336; Clinton 104; Brandt 20, 21; Shaw 274, 275; Quarles 200-205
21. Dumond 336-342; Ripley 70, 71; Clinton 104-105; Hunter 163, 164
22. Clinton105, 106; Larson 153, 154; Murray 303; *Liberty Herald*, Sept. 18, 1843.

Ten

1. GS to William H. Seward, Aug. 11, 1850, SU
2. June 19, 1873, SU
3. Frothingham, 1st ed. 114
4. 1850 U. S. census
5. *Union Herald*, Dec. 1, 1838; *Friend of Man*, Nov. 16, 1839
6. *Friend of Man*, July 2, 1839
7. Frothingham, 1sted. 190; *The Saturday Globe*, Oct. 3, 1896
8. *Albany Patriot*, June 25, 1844, 130, 131
9. Sperry 39, 51, 52
10. Loguen 401.
11. *Friend of Man*. Oct. 9, 1839
12. GS to Rev. James Smylie of Mississippi, Oct. 28, 1836, PHS
13. Sept. 2, 1896, SU
14. Quarles 157; Frothingham, 1st ed., 101
15. Gara, "The fugitive …" 236
16. Blockson, *The Underground*…98, 99
17. GS to F.B. Sanborn, Jan 29, 1861, SU.
18. Bentley 79
19. GS to F.B. Sanborn, Feb. 20, 1861; April 4, 1861, SU.
20. Larson 227; Clinton 195; *Boston Herald* 6
21. *Voice of the Fugitive*, April 9, 1851 2; Still 158; *Friend of Man*, Dec 26, 1838
22. letter, Jan 18, 1932
23. Edwards to GS, Aug. 29, 1850; July 9 1856; Sept. 8, 1856; Dec. 17, 1857; May 7, 1856

Eleven

1. Frothingham, 1st ed. 114; Stanton 51
2. *The Abolitionist*, Nov. 22, 1842 7; Mason to GS, Nov. 1, 4, 1842;

End Notes

March 15, June 30, 1843; J.B. Edwards to GS, April 29, 1852, SU
3. Clinton 86: Edwards to GS, July 17, 1845, SU
4. Nov. 27 1844 2
5. Simmonds to GS, Feb 11, July 10, 1852; Frothingham, 1st ed., 115
6. Edwards to GS, July 20, 1852, SU.
7. March 19, 1860, SU
8. Edwards to GS, Sept. 20, 1847, SU
9. *Friend of Man*, Dec. 29, 1838 1; *Union Herald*, Dec. 1, 1838
10. Vince
11. Potter to GS, printed in *The Abolitionist*, July 12, 1842 2
12. Sperry 62; William Clarke to GS, Oct. 25, 1839, SU; Loguen 370; *Friend of Man*, Nov. 6, 1839 15
13. Stanton 62, 63; Elizabeth Smith Miller to Wilbur H. Siebert, Sept. 2, 1896, SU
14. GS to William Goodell, Oct. 31 1839, SU; Federal Dana to GS, Oct. 29, 1839, SU; *Friend of Man*, April 1, 1840; Charlotte Hales to GS, Jan. 2, 1840, SU; *Friend of Man*, Nov. 6 1839 15; memorandum by William Clarke, Onondaga Historical Association
15. Van Wagenen 22
16. Van Wagenen 22; Mary Williams to Dorothy H. Willsey, Feb. 11 2004, PHS
17. "Narrative of Alexander Milton Ross" in Blockson, *The Underground* . . . 37, 38; Horton, James, *In Hope...* 233; *Canastota Bee*, Dec. 15, 1911 8
18. Decker 57; Smith pay ledgers, SU
19. *Albany Patriot*, April 22, 1846 2, 3; April 29, 1846 3; May 6, 1846 2, 3; May 20, 1846 3; Madison County Deeds, Libre BH 11, BK 417; Frothingham, 1st ed. 143
20. *Madison County Leader + Observer*, Aug. 30, 1923 5
21. Blockson, *The Underground* . . . 104; *Oneida Telegraph*, Jan. 3. 1852 3

22. *The Liberator*, Aug. 25, 1837
23. Frothingham, 1st ed. 141.
24. Roberts to GS, Aug. 8th 1837, SU
25. Seth M. Gates to GS, March 25, April 8, 1842, SU
26. Edwards to GS, Oct. 12, 1850; Feb. 1, 1851; Feb 13, 1852, SU
27. Feb 18, 1846 1
28. July 14, 1842, SU
29. Sept. 23, 1853
30. June 25, 1842, SU
31. Law and Lovejoy 1, 12, 57
32. Frothingham, 1st ed 116
33. Sept.26, 1843 3
34. Still 153
35. *The Colored American*, June 1, 1839
36. quoted in Frothingham,1st ed 120
37. Harlow 269, 270
38. S. Worthington to GS, June 6, 1841, SU; Lydia Fuller to Samuel Fuller, Sept. 7, 1841, Nomination form OMB 1024-0018, NPS; GS to Saml. Worthington, Aug 25, 1841, SU; Madison County Deeds Libre 122 BK 40
39. GS to George R. Williams in *The North Star*, Jan. 19, 1849; *Frederick Douglass' Paper*, Sept. 1, 1854
40. GS to E. Birdseye, Dec. 21, 1840, SU.
41. GS to Nathaniel Crenshaw. Dec. 30, 1841, SU.
42. SU
43. GS to E. Birdseye, July 8, 1845, SU
44. GS to Ezekiel Birdseye, July 8, 1845, SU
45. Birdseye to GS, Jan 25, 1841, SU
46. *Frederick Douglass' Paper*, June 10, 1852
47. March 31, 1847 speech in Blassingame, 40-41, 67-68
48. Nov. 6, 1844

49. G.S. Miller to Wilbur H. Siebert, Jan. 18, 1932, PHS; Van Wagenen 22; GS to Cassuis Clay, Feb. 20, 1844, SU; Harlow 274; *Voice of the Fugitive*, May 20, 1852 1

50. Bordewich, *Bound for Canaan* 333

Bibliography

Alilunas, Leo. "Fugitive Slave" cases in Ohio Prior to 1850; *Ohio Archaeological and Historical Quarterly*, 49 (1940) 160-184.

Aptheker, Herbert. *Negro Slave Revolts in the United States*, New York: International Publishers, 1939.

Bentley, Judith. *Harriet Tubman*, New York: Franklin Watts Publishers, 1990.

Blassingame, John W. editor. *The Frederick Douglass Papers*, vol. 2: 1847-54, New Haven: Yale University Press, 1982.

Blockson, Charles L. "Escape from Slavery: The Underground Railroad," *National Geographic* vol. 166, no.1, July 1984, 3-39.

Blockson, Charles. *The Underground Railroad*, New York: Prentice Hall, 1987.

Bordewich, Fergus M. *Bound for Canaan: The Underground Railroad and the War for the Soul of America*, New York: Harper Collins, 2005.

Bordewich, Fergus M. "Free at Last," *Smithsonian*, Dec. 2004 64-71.

Botkin, B. A. ed. *Lay My Burden Down: A Folk History of Slavery*, Chicago: University of Chicago Press. 1945.

Brandt, Nat. *The Town that Started the Civil War*, Syracuse: Syracuse University Press, 1990.

Campbell, Jr., Edward D.C. and Kym S. Rice, eds. *Before Freedom Came: African-American Life in the Antebellum South*, Charlottesville: University Press of Virginia, 1991.

Campbell, Stanley. *The Slave Catchers: Enforcement of the Fugitive Slave Law*, 1850-1860, New York: W. W. Norton, 1972.

Clarke, William M. *Memorandum*, Onondaga Historical Society.

Clinton, Catherine. *Harriet Tubman: The Road to Freedom*, New York: Little Brown and Company, 2004.

Decker, Frank N. *Kriemheld Herd: A Chapter in Holstein History*, Syracuse: no publisher, 1923.

Bibliography

Dillon, Merton L. *The Abolitionists*, New York: W.W. Norton & Company., 1974.

Douglass, Frederick. *My Bondage and My Freedom*, New York: Dover Publications, 1969. First published by Miller, Ortan & Mulligan, 1855.

Dumond, Dwight Lowell. *Antislavery: The Crusade for Freedom in America*, New York: W.W. Norton, 1961.

Eggert, Gerald E. "The Impact of the Fugitive Slave Law on Harrisburg: A Case Study," *Pennsylvania Magazine of History and Biography*, 109 (1985) 537-69.

Finkleman, Paul. "Prigg v Pennsylvania and Northern State Courts: Anti-Slavery use of a Pro-Slavery Decision," *Civil War History*, 25, 1979 5-35.

Fladeland, Betty. *James Gillespie Birney: Slave Holder to Abolitionist*. Ithaca: Cornell University Press, 1955.

Foner, Eric. *A Short History of Reconstruction: 1863 - 1877*. New York: Harper & Row, 1990.

Foner, Eric. *Free Soil, Free Labor, Free Men: The Ideology of the Republican Party Before the Civil War*, Oxford: Oxford University Press, 1970.

Fox, Leverett A. "Life on a Slave Ship," *The Post Standard,* Feb. 15, 2004, 43,4. First printed May 12, 1918.

Franklin, John Hope. *From Slavery to Freedom: a History of Negro Americans*, 5th edition. New York: Alfred A. Knopf, 1980.

Franklin, John Hope and Loren Schweninger. *Runaway Slaves: Rebels on the Plantation*. New York: Oxford University Press, 1999.

Frothingham, Octavius Brooks. *Gerrit Smith*, 1st ed., New York: G.P. Putman & Sons, 1877.

Gara, Larry.
- "A Glorious Time: The 1874 Abolitionist Reunion in Chicago," *Journal of Illinois Historical Society*, 65, Autumn 1972 280-292.
- "Friends and the Underground Railroad," *Quaker History*, 51, 1962 3-19.
- "Myth and Reality," in *Underground Railroad*. Washington, D.C.: Division of Publications, National Park Service, 1997.
- "The Fugitive Slave Law: A Double Paradox," *Civil War History*, 10, 1964 229-240.

Bibliography

- *The Liberty Line: The Legend of the Underground Railroad*, Lexington: University of Kentucky Press, 1961.

Gates, Henry Louis, Jr. ed. *Unchained Memories: Readings from the Slave Narratives*, New York: Bulfinch Press, 2002.

Goodheart, Lawrence B. *Abolitionist Actuary, Atheist: Elizur Wright and the Reform Impulse*, Ohio: Kent State University Press, 1990.

Groth, Michael. "Slaveholders and Manumission in Dutchess County, New York," *New York History* vol 78, no. 1, Jan. 1997 33-50.

Harlow, Ralph V. *Gerrit Smith: Philanthropist and Reformer*, New York: Henry Holt and Company. 1939.

Harrold, Stanley. *American Abolitionists*, Essex, England: Pearson Education Limited, 2001.

Higginson, Thomas Wentworth. *Contemporaries*, Boston: Houghton, Mifflin and Company, 1899.

Horton, Hayward Derrick. "Lost in the Storm: the Sociology of the Black Working Class 1850 to 1990," *American Sociological Review*, vol. 65, no.1 Feb. 2000 128-137.

Horton, James Oliver and Lois E. Horton. *Slavery and the Making of America*, New York: Oxford University Press, 2005.

Horton James Oliver and Lois E. Horton. *In Hope of Liberty: Culture, Community and Protest Among Northern Free Blacks, 1700-1860*. New York Oxford University Press, 1997.

Hunter, Carol M. *To Set the Captives Free: Reverend Jermain Wesley Loguen and the Struggle for Freedom in Central New York, 1835-1872*, New York: Garland Publishing Inc., 1993.

Johnson, Michael P. "Runaway Slaves and the Slave Communities in South Carolina, 1799 to 1830," *William and Mary Quarterly*, 38, 1981 418-41.

Kashatus, William C. *Just Over the Line: Chester County and the Underground Railroad*, University Park, Pennsylvania: Penn State University Press, 2002.

Klees, Emerson. *Underground Railroad Tales*, Rochester: Friends of the Finger Lakes Publishing, 1997.

Bibliography

Kobrin, David. *The Black Minority in Early New York*, Albany: State Education Department, 1971.

Kolchin, Peter. *American Slavery*, New York: Hill and Wang, 1993.

Larson, Kate Clifford. *Bound for the Promised Land: Harriet Tubman, Portrait of an American Hero*, New York: Ballantine Books, 2004.

Law, Robin and Paul E. Lovejoy, eds. *The Biography of Mahommah Gardo Baquaqua: His Passage from Slavery to Freedom in Africa and America*, Princeton: Markus Wiener Publishers, 2001.

Lester, Julius. *To Be a Slave*, New York: Scholastic, Inc., 1968.

Levy, Leonard W. "Sims Case: The Fugitive Slave Law in Boston in 1851." *Journal of Negro History*, 35, 1950 39-74.

Litwack, Leon F. "Slavery to Freedom," *Slavery in American Society*. Richard D. Brown, ed. Lexington: D.C. Heath, 1969.

Loguen, Jermain Wesley, as told to and written by John Thomas. *The Rev. J.W. Loguen as a Slave and as a Freeman: A Narrative of Real Life*, Syracuse: J.G.K. Truair, 1859.

Lowance, Mason, ed. *Against Slavery: An Abolitionist Reader*, New York: Penguin Books, 2000.

McFeely, William S. *Frederick Douglass,* New York: W. W. Norton, 1955.

Mabee, Carleton. *Black Freedom: The Nonviolent Abolitionists from 1830 Through the Civil War*, London: The Macmillan Company, 1970.

Madison County Deeds, Libre 11, Bk 417; Libre 122, Bk 40.

Mayer, Henry. *All On Fire: William Lloyd Garrison and the Abolition of Slavery*, New York: St. Martin's press, 1998.

Miller, John Chester. *The Wolf by the Ears: Thomas Jefferson and Slavery*, Charlottesville: University Press of Virginia, 1991.

Murray, Alexander L. "The Extradition of Fugitive Salves from Canada: A Re-evaluation," *Canadian Historical Review* 43, 1962, 298-314.

Nomination form OMB 1024-0018, NPS for the National Register of Historic Places (Internet, Feb, 2005) regarding the James C. and Lydia C. Fuller House, Skaneateles, New York.

Bibliography

Nordstrom, Carl. "The New York State Slave Code," *Afro-Americans in the New York Life and History*, 4, no 1, Jan., 1980.

Northup, Solomon. *Twelve Years a Slave*, New York: Dover Publications, 2000. First Published in 1853.

Oates, Stephen B. *The Fires of Jubilee: Nat Turner's Fierce Rebellion*, New York Harper & Row, 1975.

Osofsky Gilbert, ed. *Puttin' on Ole Massa*, New York: Harper & Row, 1969.

Painter, Nell Irvin. *Sojourner Truth: A Life, a Symbol*, W.W. Norton, 1996.

Parker Freddie L. *Running for Freedom: Slave Runaways in North Carolina 1775-1840*, New York: Garland Publishing, 1993.

Pettit, Eber. *Sketches in the History of the Underground Railroad*, Westfield, New York: Chautauqua Regional Press, 1999.

Phelan, Helene C. *And Why Not Every Man? An Account of Slavery, the Underground Railroad, and the Road to Freedom in New York's Southern Tier*, Interlaken: Heart of the Lakes Publishing, 1987.

Perry, Mark. *Lift Up Thy Voice: The Grimké Family's Journey from Slaveholders to Civil Rights Leaders*, New York: Penguin Books, 2001.

Pettit, Eber M. *Sketches in the History of the Underground Railroad*, Westfield: Chautuaqua region Press 1999 reprint. First published, 1879.

Quarles, Benjamin. *Black Abolition*, London: Oxford University Press, 1969.

Reynolds, David S. *John Brown, Abolitionist*, New York: Alfred A. Knopf, 2005.

Ripley, C. Peter; "The Underground Railroad," *Underground Railroad*, Washington, D.C.: Division of Publications, National Park Service, 1997.

Roper, Moses. *Narrative of My Escape from Slavery*, Mineola, New York: 2003. First published in 1837.

Rose, Willie Lee, ed. *A Documentary History of Slavery in North America*. Athens: The University of Georgia Press, 1999.

Bibliography

Sanborn, Franklin B. *The Life and Letters of John Brown*, Concord: F.B. Sanborn, 1885.

Scruggs, Otey. "The Meaning of Harriet Tubman", in Carol V.R. George, ed. *Remember the Ladies*, Syracuse: Syracuse University Press, 1975.

Sernett, Milton. *North Star Country*, Syracuse: Syracuse University Press, 2002.

Sewell, Richard H. *Ballots for Freedom: Antislavery Politics in the United States 1837-1860*, New York: Oxford University Press, 1976.

Shaw, Robert B. *A Legal History of Slavery in the Unites States*, Potsdam: Northern Press, 1991.

Smith Gerrit. Address to the New York State Abolition Convention, January, 1842.

Smith, William Henry. *A Political History of Slavery*, New York: Frederick Ungar 1966. First published in 1903.

Sperry, Earl E. *The Jerry Rescue: October 1, 1851*, Syracuse: Onondaga Historical Society, 1924.

Stampp, Kenneth M. ed. *The Causes of the Civil War*, 3rd revised ed., New York: Simon & Schuster, 1991.

Stampp, Kenneth. *The Peculiar Institution: Slavery in the Anti-Bellum South*, New York: Alfred A. Knopf, 1956.

Stampp, Kenneth M. "Rebels and Sambos: The Search for the Negro's Personality in Slavery," *Journal of Southern History*, 37, 1971 367-392.

Stanton, Elizabeth Cady. *Eighty Years and More*, New York: Schocken Books, 1971. First published in 1896.

Sterling, Dorothy, *Ahead of Her Time: Abby Kelley and the Politics of Antislavery*, New York: W. W. Norton & Co., 1991.

Stevenson, Brenda E. "Slavery in America," *Underground Railroad*, Washington, D.C.: Division of Publications, National Park Service. 1997.

Steward, Austin. *Twenty-Two Years a Slave and Forty Years a Freeman*, Syracuse, NY: Syracuse University Press, 2002. First published in 1857.

Bibliography

Still, William. *The Underground Railroad*, New York: Arno Press, 1968. First published in 1872.

Sturge, Joseph. *A Visit to the United States in 1841*, London: Hamilton Adams & Co., 1842. Reprinted by Augustus M. Kelley Publishers, New York, 1969.

Tate, Thad W. *The Negro in Eighteenth Century Williamsburg*, Williamsburg: The Colonial Williamsburg Foundation, 1965.

Thornbrough, Emma Lou. "Indiana and Fugitive Slave Legislation," *Indiana Magazine of History*, 50, 1954 201-228.

Turner, Edward Raymond. "The Underground Railroad in Pennsylvania," *Pennsylvania Magazine of History and Biography*, 36, 1912 309-318.

United States Census, 1850.

Van Wagenen, Jared. "The Story of Gerrit Smith: Reflections from a Visit to a Home Where History Was Made," *American Agriculturalist*, Dec. 3, 1927 22.

Vince, Thomas L. "Chaplain's Call to Glory began at WRA," *Preserve Alumni Record*, Fall, 2002.

Weld, Theodore Dwight. *American Slavery as it is: Testimony of a Thousand Witnesses*, New York: The American Anti-Slavery Society, 1839.

Wiecek, William M. *The Sources of Antislavery Constitutionalism in America, 1760-1848*, Ithaca: Cornell University Press, 1977.

Wilson, Benjamin C. "Kentucky Kidnappers Fugitives and Abolitionists in Antebellum Cass County Michigan," *Michigan History* 60, 1976 339-358.

Wiltsie, Charles M. ed. *David Walker's Appeal*, New York: Hill and Wang, 1965.

Wish, Harvey. *George Fitzhugh: Propagandist of the Old South*, Louisiana State University Press, 1943.

Yanuch, Julius. "The Garner Fugitive Slave Case," *Mississippi Valley Historical Review* 40, 1953 47-66.

Yetman, Norman R., ed. *When I was a Slave: Memoirs from the Slave Narrative Collection*, Mineola: Dover Publications, 2002.

Bibliography

Periodicals

Albany Patriot, Nov 27, 1844; Feb. 18, 1846; April 22, 29, 1846; May 6, 20, 1846.

Boston Herald, "The Underground Railroad." Special section, March 3, 1971.

Canastota Bee, Dec 15, 1911.

Frederick Douglass' Paper, Sept.1, 1854; June 10, 1852; Sept 23, 1853.

Friend of Man, June 23, 1836; July 21, 28, 1836; Sept. 1, 27, 1836; Oct. 1, 1836; Dec. 26, 29, 1838; Oct. 9, 1839; Nov 6, 1839; Feb. 8, 1840; April 1, 1840; May 27, 1843.

The Abolitionist, July 12, 1842; Nov. 22, 1842.

The Colored American, June 1, 1839.

The Freeholder, April 29, 1809.

The Liberator, Jan.5, 1838; Jan.18, 1839; Nov. 30, 1849; July 28, 1861.

The Lily, "Glen Haven Water Cure," August, 1852.

The North Star, Jan 19, 1849.

The Saturday Globe, Oct. 3, 1896.

Toronto Globe, Oct. 15, 1850.

Liberty Herald, Nov. 16, 1843; Sept. 14, 1843.

Liberty Press, June 20, 1843; Sept. 26, 1843.

Madison County Leader & Observer, Aug. 30, 1923.

Madison Observer, Nov. 29, 1843.

Oneida Telegraph, Jan.3, 1852.

Voice of the Fugitive, April 9, 1851; May 20, 1852.

Index

10th New York Cavalry 124

A

Adams, Louisa 43
African Methodist Church of Boston 97
Agriculture 20
Alabama
 19, 38, 43, 44, 52, 64
Albany, NY
 76, 105, 112, 124
Albany Patriot 116, 127
American Revolution 8
American ships 14
Anderson (slave) 130
Antebellum era
 30, 39, 85, 132
Antebellum South 26
Anti-Fugitive Slave Law Convention In Cazenovia, NY 77, 78
Arkansas 19

B

Baptist Colored Church of Buffalo 99
Baquaquam, Mahommah Gardoi 129
Beck, Isaac 70
Beecher, Charles 89
Bethel, Austin 126
Bethel Town 127
Bibb, Henry 27
Binghamton, NY
 105, 118, 129
Birdseye, Ezekiel 134
Birney, James G.
 11, 36, 57
Bliss, Lyman 124
Bloodhound Bill 92
Boone County, KY 87
Booth, Joseph 70
Boston 78
Boston Tea Party 109
Bradford, Sarah 113
Branding 55
Braxton, Carter 132
Br'er Rabbit 45
Britain 67, 76, 97
British Empire 97
British Parliament 14
British ships 14
Brown, John 58
Brown, William Wells
 51, 76
Buchanan, James 30
Buffalo, NY 76
Buxton, Ont. 97
Byrd II, William 23

C

Calkins, Caleb
 106, 136, 137
Canada
 19, 20, 58, 76, 80, 96, 97, 99, 100, 105, 107, 108, 111, 112, 113, 116, 122, 126, 129, 130, 136
Canastota, NY 124
Captain Aaron Bliss 124
Caribbean Sea 13
Carter, Robert 56
Catskill Mountains 104
Cazenovia, NY 109
Centerville, NY 34
Central America 13
Central New York 106, 116
Chambersburg, PA 129
Channing, William Ellery 24
Chapman, Maria 78

When We Get to Heaven

Chatham, Ont. 99
Chester County, PA 112
Child, Lydia Maria 32, 33
Christian churches 35
Christiana, PA 86
Christmas 42
Christmas Eve 80
Cincinnati 19, 87
Cincinnati Gazette 25
Civil War
    30, 36, 68, 80, 85, 97, 120, 124
Clark County, VA 127
Clark, Lewis 130
Clarke, Dr. John 120
Clarke, William 120
Cleveland 99
Clinton, NY 120
Cobb, Thomas 51
Coffin, Levi 79
Coffle 38
Colchester, Ont. 97
Colored Baptist Church of Rochester 99
Colorphobia 96
Compromise of 1850 92
Concordia Parish, LA 64
Congress 18, 30, 35
Congressman William Smith 18
Connecticut 20
Conscious accommodation 46
Cook, John F. 127
Cortland, NY 113
Cortlandville, NY 118
Cottage Across the Brook 133
Cotton 41
Cotton fields 40
Cotton gin 7, 63

D

Dana, Federal 106, 121, 122
Darwin, Charles 30

Davis, David Brion 45
Davis, Jefferson 23, 24
Dawn, Ont. 99
Declaration of Independence 7, 27, 57
Delaware 70
Denmark, IA 87
Denmark Vesey plot 59, 61
Detroit 83, 97
Dominion Bank 96
Dorsey (slave) 116
Douglass, Frederick
    8, 9, 25, 28, 37, 39, 40, 45, 52, 62, 72, 76, 77, 78, 93, 95, 105, 112, 125, 127, 135
Dunbar, William 57

E

Education of slaves 51
Edwards, John B.
    106, 113, 116, 117, 126
Elgin, Ont. 99
Emancipation 69
England 73
Epps plantation 55
Erie Canal 129
Essay on Slavery 24
Europe 37

F

Farmers & Exchange Bank of Charleston, SC 41
Farmers Bank of Missouri 41
Faussitt, William 70
Female Anti-slavery Society of Rochester, NY 28
First Baptist Church of Boston 97
Fitzhugh, Henry 129
Fitzhugh, William 124
Flores, Joe 8, 28, 33, 105
Florida 19
Forten, James 95, 96
Fourth of July 28, 29

Index

France 19
Franklin, John Hope 10
Free African Society 76
Freeman, Walter 127
Friend of Man 122
Frothingham, O.B. 115, 124
Fugitive Aid Society 76
Fugitive Slave Act 98
Fugitive Slave Bill 106
Fugitive Slave Law
   63, 68, 75, 90, 91,
   92, 93, 97, 126
Fuller, James Canning
   132, 133

G

Gabriel plot 59, 61
Gap Gang 86
Garner, Margaret 87
Garnet, Henry Highland
   62, 76, 78, 105
Garrett, Thomas
   81, 112, 123
Garrison, William Lloyd
   27, 28, 32, 58, 61, 78, 125
Garrisonian abolitionists
   78
Georgia 15, 19, 40, 119
Gerrit Smith Estate-
   National Historic Landmark 106, 108, 134, 135
Gibbons, Daniel 75
Golden Rule 17, 70
Gorsuch, Edward 86
Gradual Emancipation
   Society of
   North Carolina 51
Great Dismal Swamp 82
Grimke, Angelina
   11, 33, 49
Grimke, Sarah 49
Grimke sisters 36
Gudger, Sara 42

H

Hagerstown, MD 129, 131
Hales, Charlotte 122
Hammond, Congressman Jabez E. 58
Harper, William 30
Harpers Ferry, raid on 58
Harris, Kim 94
Harris, Reggie 94
Harrisburgh, PA 129
Harrison, Samuel 119
Hayden, Lewis 35
Heaven 37, 56, 93, 100, 105
Higginson, Thomas Wentworth 68
Hitchcock, Peter 113
Hockley, Benjamin 126

I

Illinois Gov. John L. Beveridge 68
Independence Day 27, 28
Indiana 79

J

Jackson, James Caleb
   76, 124
Jackson, Martin 61
Jacobs, Harriet 24, 47, 62
James River, Virginia 6
Jefferson, Thomas
   7, 26, 32, 57
Jerry Rescue 80, 109, 110
Johnson, Abraham 128
Johnson, Daniel 128
Johnson, Franklin 128
Johnson, Jack 128
Jonesborough, Tennessee 58

K

Kellogg, Hiram 103
Kelly, Henry 122
Kentucky
   25, 35, 36, 51, 70, 130

When We Get to Heaven

King George III of England 57
Kingston, Ont. 122
Ku Klux Klan 85

L

Ladies' Aid Societies 80
Lagrow, John 129
Lake Erie 6, 97, 99
Lake Ontario 94
Lanfrey, Pierre 7
Lawrence, James R. 109
Lebanon, NY 120
Lee, William 131, 132
Legree, Simon 53
Lewis, Lovinla 127
Liberty 27
Liberty Herald 136
Liberty Party 90, 124
Liberty Party Convention 109
Logue, Jarm 24
Loguen, Jermain Wesley 24, 25, 54, 69, 72, 76, 80, 86, 94, 99, 109, 113, 120, 130
London, England 24, 135
Louisiana Purchase 19

M

Madison County 104, 107, 124, 130
Madison County Historical Society 77
Manumission 20, 69
Marks, William 83
Marshall, James 87
Maryland 15, 20, 25, 63, 70, 83, 89, 123, 124, 128
Maryland Gazette 70
Maryland law 18
Mason, John Thomson 116, 128, 131
Mason, Sen. James 92
Massachusetts 20, 76, 93

May, Samuel J. 75, 113
Maysville, KY 130
Mechanicsburg, Ohio 82
Mexico 58
Meyers, Stephen 76
Michigan 99
Miller, Elizabeth Smith 111
Miller, Gerrit Smith 113, 123, 124, 133, 136
Mississippi 19
Montreal 99
Morville Plantation 64
Mott, Lucretia Coffin 125
Murder of slaves 40

N

Naples, NY 83
Nat Turner rebellion 59, 61
National Abolition Hall of Fame & Museum 8, 28, 33, 105, 125, 140
National Anti-Slavery Reunion in Chicago 68
National Historic Landmark 108
Native Americans 30, 71
New England 20
New Hampshire 20
New Jersey 20, 80
New Orleans 82, 117, 123
New York 20, 71, 82, 113
New York Central College 129
New York City 16, 20, 135
New York City Vigilance Committee 86
New York State laws 21
New York State Abolition Convention 107
New York State Anti-Slavery Society 58, 119
New York State Assembly 112

Index

New York State Vigilance Committee 76, 109, 111
New York Tribune 25
Newport, IN 79
North Carolina 19, 43, 58, 59. 82, 85, 89, 90, 126
North Carolina Supreme Court 51
North Star, The 81
Northup, Solomon 34, 40, 41, 42, 43, 52, 55, 57, 85

O

Ocean journey 13
Ohio 25, 75, 79, 82, 90
Ohio Underground Railroad 70
Oneida, NY 124
Onondaga Historical Association 54
Ontario 97
Orange County, OH 136
Oswego County Historical Society 117
Oswego, NY 105, 106, 113, 116, 117, 126, 129, 136
Overseer 40, 41, 52
Oxford, PA 85

P

Pennsylvania 20, 71, 73, 91, 113, 123
Pennsylvania Anti-Slavery Society 80
Pennsylvania Society for the Promotion of the Abol 95
Peterboro Manual Labor School 119
Peterboro, NY 36, 76, 100, 103, 104, 105, 106, 113, 115, 116, 117, 118,119, 123, 126, 132, 133, 136
Philadelphia 76, 80, 95, 96, 113, 130
Plantation 45
Plantation life 37
Potter, Thomas 120
Powell, Harriet 120, 121
President Millard Fillmore 92
Prigg v Pennsylvania 91
Pro-slavery policies 35
Proctor, Jenny 44, 52, 62
Purvis, Robert 96

Q

Quakers 18, 71, 79, 96
Queen Victoria 127

R

Republican Party 25, 36
Revolutionary War 32
Reynolds, Mary 39
Rhode Island 20, 93
Riots 19
Robert (slave) 130
Roberts, John 126
Rochester, NY 28, 76, 112
Roman law 16
Roper, Moses 69
Ross, Alexander Milton 123
Ruggles, David 76
Russel, Bill 125
Russell family 134
Russell, Harriet 133, 135
Russell, Malvina "Vinny" 133

S

Sanborn, Franklin Benjamin 68
Saratoga, NY 85
Scott, John W. 118

When We Get to Heaven

Second Great Awakening
   21, 58
Sedgwick, Charles B. 113
Self-mutilation 46
Shenandoah County, Virginia
   15
Siebert, Wilbur H.
   111, 113
Simmonds, L.E. 117
Simpson, Ben 40
Skaneateles, NY 132
Slave collars 38
Slave culture 26
Slave health 43
Slave marriages 39
Slave Power 17, 35, 36, 92
Slave punishment
   52, 53, 55, 56
Slave quarters 45
Slave rations 42
Slave rebellions
   20, 57, 58, 59, 61
Slave resistance
   46, 47, 48, 49, 50
Slave suicides 69, 87
Smith, Alden Maxwell
   124, 125
Smith, Ann Fitzhugh
   106, 126, 129, 132, 136
Smith, Billy 124, 125
Smith, Elizabeth 106, 121
Smith, Gerrit
   11, 58, 68, 76, 77, 78, 79,
   82, 99, 100, 103, 106,
   107, 109, 110, 112, 113,
   115, 116, 119, 122, 125,
   130, 132, 135, 137
Smith, Greene 106, 112
Smith, Rev. Phineas 34
South America 13
South Carolina
   18, 19, 36, 59, 84, 85, 122
South Carolina Supreme
   Court 51
Southampton County, VA 59
Southern children 27

Southern economy 25
St. Catherine's 99
St. Michael's 25
Stable barn, Peterboro
   108, 138
Stanton, Elizabeth Cady
   115, 121
Station masters 79
Steward, Austin 52
Stewart, Alvan 90
Still, William 80, 82, 113
Sturge, Joseph 79
Swain, Moses 51
Syracuse, NY 24, 54, 76,
   80, 99, 109, 113, 120,
   121, 122, 129, 130

T

Tappan, Arthur 135
Tappan brothers 76
Tennessee
   15, 71, 80, 126, 134
The Brookes 14
The drinkin' gourd 64, 81
The Freeholder 103
The Laundry 135
The Liberator 58, 96
Thompson, Robert 118
Three-fifths rule 35
Tobacco 6
Tocqueville, Alexis de 33
Toronto 129
Toronto Globe 97
Town of Smithfield 103
Trowbridge, Theron 87
Troy, NY 76, 105
Tubman, Harriet
   5, 68, 83, 94, 99,
   112, 113, 116, 121, 125
Twelfth Baptist Church of
   Boston 97
Tyler, John 123

Index

U

U.S. Constitution
  7, 17, 27, 35, 36, 90
U.S. Supreme Court 91
Uncle Tom's Cabin 53
Underground Railroad
  54, 62, 64, 68, 69,
  70, 71, 75, 79, 80,
  81, 83, 99, 100, 104,
  111, 112, 113, 115, 123,
  124, 126, 130, 137
United States
  24, 41, 59, 68, 79,
  96, 97, 105, 122, 136
Utica, NY 119, 130

V

Vermont 20
Virginia
  6, 15, 30, 59, 61, 63,
  82, 83, 95, 96, 124, 126, 132
Virginia law 18, 19

W

Walker, Jonathan 93
Walkers' Appeal 90
Walls, George 85
Ward, Margaret 124
Ward, Samuel 124
Ward, Samuel Ringgold 96
Washington, Catharine 124

Washington, D.C.
  85, 127, 134
Washington, George 10
Washington, Julia Lewis
  124
Washington, Lewis 124
Watertown, NY 122
Watkins, Robert H. 43
Webster, Charles 103
Weedon, George 126
Weld, Theodore
  33, 34, 43, 49, 50
Western Hemisphere 13
Western Reserve Academy
  119
Whip 40, 67, 84
Whipping scars 70, 118
Whippings 55
Whitney, Eli 7
Whittier, John Greenleaf
  73, 93
Wilberforce, Ont. 99
Wilberforce settlement 19
Wilkesbarre, PA 129
Williams, George R. 134
Williams, Hanson 124
Williams, Jim 84
Williams, John 118
Williams, Mary 123
Williamsburg, VA 62
Wilmington, DE 112
Windsor, Ont. 96, 97
Wright, H. C. 45

About the Author

Norman K. Dann, Ph.D. was born in Providence, RI in 1940. After graduating from Mt. Pleasant High School, he spent three years in the U.S. Navy as an aviation electronics technician.

He earned a B.A. degree in psychology from Alderson-Broaddus College in Philippi, WV and an M.A. in Political Science at the University of Rhode Island.

He was graduated from Syracuse University in 1974 with a Ph.D. in Interdisciplinary Social Sciences. In 1999, he retired after 33 years on the faculty of the Social Sciences Department at Morrisville College in Central New York.

"I never had a bad day at work as a faculty member," he says.

In retirement, Norm has specialized in research and writing on the abolition movement, with several articles and book reviews for publication. His second book, a biography of Gerrit Smith, is due in 2009.

His other interests include Sterling silver craft work. He creates jewelry pieces and specializes in silver plaques that commemorate the histories of towns, villages, and other municipalities. One plaque was a centerpiece of the 2006 celebration of Madison County's bicentennial. Norm also enjoys archery hunting for whitetail deer and maintains a large vegetable garden. He cultivates hop plants for display and sale through the annual Madison County Hop Fest.

Norm has dedicated his retirement to communicating the importance of local history regarding abolition. He is a member of the Peterboro-based Smithfield Community Association and helps manage the group's annual fund-raiser, Civil War Weekend. He is a founding member of the National Abolition Hall of Fame and serves on its Cabinet of Freedom.